Living Cruelty Free

Living Cruelty Free

Published by:
Greatest Guides Limited, Woodstock, Bridge End, Warwick
CV34 6PD, United Kingdom

www.greatestguides.com

Greatest Guides is committed to a sustainable future for our
planet. This book is printed on paper certified by the Forest
Stewardship Council.

FSC FSC® C020837
MIX
Paper

Printed and bound in the United Kingdom

ISBN 978-1-907906-22-0

Acknowledgements

I would like to thank the following for their invaluable help with this book.

My partner John, who helped me with the picture research, and who acted as a soundboard for content ideas.

My fellow tweeters on Twitter, who helped clarify in my mind what needed to be included in this book.

My friends on Facebook, who also helped me decide on the content.

All of the charities working for the welfare of people and animals who gave me permission to use quotes and offered me advice. Special thanks to the BUAV, for allowing me to use the world famous cruelty free Leaping Bunny mark.

Contents

A few words from Jennifer…

The very fact you've picked up this book means you want to live a more compassionate lifestyle; one that is kind to people and animals. This could be because you are a vegetarian or vegan and want to avoid things that involve the harming or killing of animals, whether it's for meat or cosmetics.

Or, maybe you are a meat-eater and simply want to ensure that the animals that end up on your plate had a good quality of life before they died and were allowed to roam freely and feel the sun on their faces.

Perhaps you are simply looking to be a more ethical shopper, shunning goods made in sweatshops or using exploited child labor.

Yes, trying to live a cruelty free life means human beings are treated well too – just as Ghandi said, you can judge a society by how it treats animals, we can also judge our society by how people treat their fellow human beings.

No matter how far you want to go in the pursuit of a more compassionate lifestyle, the pages of this book will arm you with the facts you need to make an informed decision about the things you buy and the things you eat.

Remember, together, with small steps, we can all make the world a kinder place to live.

How to read this book

This book can be read cover to cover and as a reference guide to dip into again and again.

If you have any questions, please feel free to contact me through my blog at **http://greatestguidetolivingcrueltyfree.blogspot.com**

Jennifer

What Is Cruelty Free?

" The human spirit is not dead. It lives on in secret.... It has come to believe that compassion, in which all ethics must take root, can only attain its full breadth and depth if it embraces all living creatures and does not limit itself to mankind. "

Albert Schweitzer, Nobel Peace winner in 1952, medical missionary, humanitarian and nuclear disarmament advocate

Chapter 1
What Is Cruelty Free?

WHAT IS CRUELTY FREE?

We all think we know what it means, but sometimes it can be difficult to define.

For the purposes of this book, living cruelty free is defined as causing no harm to animals or humans.

This can mean a number of things:

- Not buying food that was produced by causing unnecessary suffering to animals, such as placing animals in small, darkened crates where they live out their short lives without any contact with their own kind (this is how calves used to make veal live to ensure their meat is pale).

- Not buying products that are made from the labor of workers who are not adequately paid for the work they do or treated fairly. This can mean they live in squalid, unsanitary conditions (such as having no fresh water) and are not paid a fair wage for the work they do.

- Not buying cosmetics that are tested on animals. Many of these tests are completely unnecessary and have been done countless times before, so they already know what the results will be.

- Not buying things that were made using obvious animal cruelty. This can mean not buying things like pillows and bedding that contain duck feathers or down, which is often obtained by the plucking of animals whilst they are still alive, without anesthetic, and fur.

- Not buying clothing made by child slave labor. Firms have been found using child labor to make everything from dresses to footballs. Generally, these children never go to school.

Note – The key thing about being cruelty free is that you can go as far as you want. Every little helps.

WHY DO PEOPLE DECIDE TO SHOP CRUELTY FREE?

You may be a vegetarian or vegan and want to avoid all products that are by-products of the slaughterhouse, such as gelatin (also spelt gelatine) in candies (sweets) and lambskin and products that are tested on animals.

Even if you're not a vegetarian or a meat reducer, without even realizing it, you may have already taken steps to become a cruelty free shopper. Perhaps you have a conscientious objection to buying certain products. Say you love horses and avoid anything that contains horse hair or anything that is made with deerskin because you think of Bambi. Or, maybe you don't eat certain things because of the cruelty involved or because they remind you of the animal it came from.

Whatever the reason, there is a rise in the number of consumers who care how products are made and how they are sourced. That's why products carry labels saying they are cruelty free or ethically sourced, or are made by workers who are paid a fair wage. If these guarantees weren't demanded by the public, they wouldn't be there, as businesses simply want to make as much money as possible. They may herald their ethical policies, but, in most cases, they don't want to change the world. They just want to cash in on new trends in consumer behavior.

WHY SHOULD I BECOME A CRUELTY FREE SHOPPER?

There are a number of reasons:

- Because you want to know the things you buy didn't involve cruelty towards people or animals.

" Everyone thinks of changing the world, but no one thinks of changing himself. "

Tolstoy

- You want to know that you are doing your bit to help make the world a place where human beings and animals are shown compassion and understanding.

- The more people who buy cruelty free products, the more common cruelty free products will become. For instance, the public's anger about the testing of cosmetics on animals in the 1980's led to a number of companies shunning animal testing in favor of more reliable methods of testing products, like doing skin tests on the humans who would actually be using them. This made products that were not tested on animals more readily available. What the customer demands, the customer gets.

- If shoppers shunned cruel products then those products would no longer exist. If companies found that cruelty free products were what made them the most profit then that is what they would sell.

- You want to leave a kinder world for your children.

- To make a difference.

CAN I REALLY MAKE A DIFFERENCE?

Hearing about all the bad things that happen in the world can leave us in a state of despair. How can we, as individuals, stop all the bad things from happening: put an end to all the cruelty and misery people and animals suffer from every single day?

The answer is that we can't. What we can do is change how we behave and live a more compassionate life, and, where we see things we don't approve of, speak up. If everybody did that, we could all change the world together.

Here are some examples of people power that did make a difference:

- It was South Africa being shunned by the international community via sanctions that led to the end of apartheid; the system whereby the majority of the population, who were black, were discriminated against by the government. No military action was proposed or needed.

- In 2002, after public outrage, the USA banned the importing, exporting, sale and production of cat and dog fur. This came about after stores unknowingly sold cat and dog fur in jackets.
  Note – the fur ban only applies to cat and dog fur and not any other type.

- Fur farming is now banned in the UK. This followed successful campaigning by animal welfare campaigners and came at a time when 76 percent of people in the UK opposed the trade.

- In response to a 2003 campaign by Animal Aid, Focus (a UK DIY store chain) announced that it would no longer sell live animals (like fish) in its stores.

- Fairtrade (known as Fairtrade certified in the USA and Canada) ensures that workers are treated and paid fairly and is one of the fastest growing brands in the world. This has come about because of the desire of millions of people to buy products that don't involve slave labor or workers living in appalling conditions.

- There was public outrage when a TV documentary showed children making clothes in Indian refugee camps. Hundreds of people protested outside Primark's Oxford Street store and it was all over the media. As a result, the store sacked three of its suppliers.

- In 2005, Inditex, who owned fashion chain Zara, agreed to withdraw fur from all of its 2,054 stores in 52 different countries. This followed a campaign by the Coalition to Abolish the Fur Trade (CAFT).

- In 2011, pop star Morrissey agreed to play at Belgian musical festival Lokerse Feesten if they banned horse-meat from their stalls. They agreed and out went the horse-meat (horse-meat is a delicacy in Belgian) and in came tofu and hummus.

- In 2011, designer label Versace banned the sandblasting technique for 'killer' jeans after pressure from activists. Sandblasting involves firing tiny particles of silica at the fabric to create a worn and faded look. If inhaled, Silica can cause silicosis, a pulmonary disease that can make workers ill and even kill them. Many other leading brands, such as Benneton, Levi Strauss, Pepe and Burberry, had already banned sandblasted jeans. The Clean Clothes Campaign (CCC) had called for the technique to be banned. Read more about CCC and their work at **www.cleanclothes.org**.

WHAT DO I NEED TO DO TO BECOME A CRUELTY FREE SHOPPER?

The most important thing shoppers need is information. Without being informed, how can we possibly know which things involve cruelty?

For instance, nobody knew that items of clothing were being made with dog and cat fur from so called factories in China, until it was revealed in the media. Prior to that, most people assumed the 'fur' trim on coats was fake fur and not the real thing.

DO YOU NEED TO BE VEGETARIAN OR VEGAN TO BE CRUELTY FREE?

Ideally, not eating meat or consuming any by-products from the meat industry is a more compassionate way to live, but you can still live a kinder life without being vegetarian or vegan. Say by choosing not to eat lobster (lobsters are thrown into boiling water alive and there is scientific evidence that they do feel pain) and Foie gras (produced by force-feeding geese and ducks until their livers expand to many times their natural size – **see Chapter 2 Things that can never be cruelty free.**)

HOW FAR DO I NEED TO GO TO BE CRUELTY FREE?

Small changes, like not going to circuses with live animals and adopting a dog instead of buying a puppy, can make a real difference (See **Chapter 7 19 Ways to Create a More Compassionate World**). So too can having your dog neutered so that you're not adding to the problem of there being too many dogs and not enough homes.

HOW TO SPOT CRUELTY FREE PRODUCTS

Cruelty free shoppers are avid readers of labels and packing. They look for things on labels like:

- fairtrade (also Fair Trade).

- ethically sourced.

- cruelty free – there is a Leaping Bunny logo on products to show that neither they nor their ingredients were tested on animals.

- not tested on animals – this doesn't guarantee the ingredients weren't tested on animals, either by the company selling the product or their suppliers.

- recycled/recyclable.

- environmentally friendly.

- vegetarian/vegan.

- free-range – this means something different depending on what country you're in.

- made from sustainable materials.

- organic (this is kinder to the environment, humans and animals).

" Love and compassion are necessities, not luxuries. Without them humanity cannot survive. "

Dalai Lama

ARE CRUELTY FREE PRODUCTS SAFE IF THEY'RE NOT TESTED ON ANIMALS?

Chemists know exactly what ingredients will interact safely with one another and cause allergic reactions in humans. They would never risk selling unsafe products because they would end up being sued.

And just because products and ingredients aren't tested on animals doesn't mean they aren't tested at all. Non-animal methods are used, like skin patch testing on human volunteers or on human skin and cell cultures made in a test tube. Computer generated models are also used.

I CAN'T AFFORD TO GO CRUELTY FREE

Just because products are cruelty free does not necessary mean they will be more expensive. In fact, in many cases, such as with cosmetics, the products produced without animal testing are often cheaper than ones that are tested on animals. This is because it costs vast sums of money to test on animals. You need laboratories, researchers and special equipment.

Some discount stores or supermarkets' own brand cosmetics and products will be cruelty free, such as Superdrug in the UK, or they may sell cheap brands that are cruelty free. If you can't get cruelty free cosmetics in store, there are dozens of online stores you can buy from. Their products are often cheaper than they would be in regular stores. You can also buy from eBay, where products are often sold at a discount, especially when they are the last in a line of stock.

In the case of food, things that involve animal cruelty, like veal and Foie gras, are very expensive to buy.

WILL PEOPLE THINK I'M STRANGE?

These days it's not unusual for people to be more interested in what they buy and where it comes from. You will not be alone in wanting to be a more compassionate shopper. Here are some facts:

- It used to be the case that cruelty free cosmetics were hard to find, but, because of consumer demand, that is no longer the case. Have a look in your local drugstore or mall and you will see that not being tested on animals is seen as a good sales tool.

- Major US food companies, like Kellogg (they bought vegetarian food label Worthington Foods and have the Morningstar Farms brand, which is meatless), Kraft Foods (they have vegetarian Boca Foods) and Dean Foods (they bought soy/Soya milk company White Wave) have either created their own line of meat substitutes or have bought companies that produce vegetarian foods. This is to cope with the demand as Americans move towards a more meatless diet.

- In 2010, despite the economic downturn, spending on green products and services went up by 18 percent in the UK. Fairtrade food sales rose from 64 percent. Source – The Co-operative Bank's annual Ethical Consumerism Report.

- In the UK, frozen meat substitute sales accounted for 73 percent of vegetarian food sales between 2001 and 2003. Source – market research firm Mintel.

But, if anyone does think it's strange that you care about the origins of the things you buy, ask yourself this: how can showing compassion for other human beings and animals be considered strange?

Isn't it our compassion for other living things that defines our humanity?

Shouldn't it be not showing compassion that's considered strange?

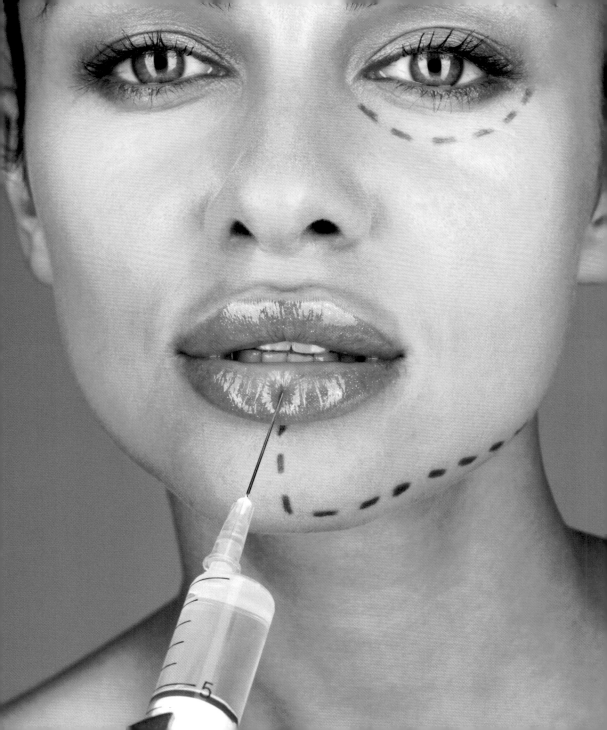

Things That Can Never Be Cruelty Free

" If a group of beings from another planet were to land on Earth… beings who considered themselves as superior to you as you feel yourself to be to other animals… would you concede them the rights over you that you assume over other animals? "

George Bernard Shaw, playwright, Nobel Prize 1925

Chapter 2

Things That Can Never Be Cruelty Free

There are certain things that under no circumstances can be described as cruelty free.

BOTOX

The increased popularity of Botox (Botulinium) injections has led to a sharp increase in the number of LD50 (LD stands for lethal dose) tests being carried out on mice. In these tests, mice are injected with Botox, which is a toxin that causes paralysis and, eventually, death by suffocation.

For each batch, a hundred mice are poisoned and observed for days. The test is carried out to see how much of the toxin it takes to kill half of the mice. Hence LD50 – a lethal dose that kills 50 percent of test subjects. This is supposed to help determine a safe dose for human use, but mice are not humans and the reliability of these tests has been called into question.

There are non-animal tests that are considered to be more reliable, but, until they come into widespread usage, Botox is not cruelty free. This is because when licenses are given for Botox toxicity testing, NO distinction is made between batches intended for the cosmetic and pharmaceutical sector (Botox does have medical uses). This way, even when it's used for cosmetics (non-medical reasons), companies manage to completely bypass the ban on testing cosmetics on animals.

CHINESE MEDICINE CONTAINING ANIMAL PARTS

Medicines will often contain bones from endangered animals, like tigers (their powdered bone is used in many different concoctions) and from domestic animals, like dogs, cows and goats. Products may also contain rhino, leopard, shark and bear (bear farming was introduced in 1984 – bears are put in tiny cages and their bile is extracted through catheters, which is very painful). These animals are farmed so they can be killed and used in Chinese medicines.

Note – Not all Chinese medicines contain animal parts, some are based on plants. If you visit a practitioner and want to know what's in their medicine, always ask. You have a right to know what you are putting in your body.

fact

In 1993, China banned the trade in tiger bones. This was because the species was heading for extinction unless something was done. In 2007, under pressure from tiger farm owners, the government lifted part of the trade ban on parts from farmed tigers. The lifting of the ban was opposed by tiger conservation groups around the world, as well as many of China's neighbors.

fact

Shark cartilage is touted as a cancer cure in Chinese medicine, but there is no proof that this is the case.

tip

Some beauty remedies, such as creams, may contain shark cartilage, as do some alternative medicines and vitamin supplements.

fact

The practice of finning is banned in the USA, but the sale of shark fins is not. In 2010, Hawaii banned people from possessing, selling, trading and distributing shark fins.

CRABS

Like **Lobsters** (see further down), crabs die painful deaths, usually by being thrown into scalding water and boiled alive, if they are not electrocuted, micro-waved or chopped up whilst still alive. That's if they survive being caught by fishermen.

Many crabs die in fishermen's nets by having their claws torn off, or through injuries they get from other crabs who, in such a confined space, will panic and fight with them.

fact

During the cooking process, crabs will battle to escape, breaking off their claws as they do and causing themselves more injuries.

DOWN (sometimes called feather down, duck down or goose down). It may be well known that fur production is cruel (for more details, go down to 'Fur'), but what many people don't know is that goose and duck down involves animal cruelty.

Down, the soft feathers closest to a bird's body, is used in blankets, coats, jackets, comforters, quilts, pillows and even upholstered furniture. It's well known for its warmth quality. Well, it is there to keep birds warm, especially in winter.

There are two ways these feathers are obtained. Firstly, the birds may have already been killed for meat production and are then plucked, but the most painful way is by plucking their feathers whilst they are still alive. This is called 'live plucking.'

There is no way to tell what method has been used, unless the product proudly boasts of the animal still being alive when it was de-feathered, which rarely happens.

This practice was first brought to the public's attention by a Swedish documentary in 2009. Showing a Hungarian goose farm where the practice was used, audiences were shocked by the sight of birds having their feathers ripped off. Many ended up paralyzed and some were left with gaping wounds, which were then cruelly sewn up by workers who didn't use any pain medication on the birds.

In China, Poland and Hungary the practice of live plucking goes on all the time, as the quality of the down is thought to be better when taken from live birds. Many of these birds are then used for Foie gras production (for more information on that, go down to '**Foie Gras**').

In America, live plucking is not an industry method, but the US does import from countries who use this practice.

fact

It's estimated that as much as 50-80% of down on sale comes from birds who have had the feathers ripped from their bodies whilst they are still alive.

fact

There are alternatives to down. Things like Thinsulate (commonly used in hats and other outerwear), Thermolite and Primaloft. All are synthetic and that means cruelty free.

FOIE GRAS (pronounced 'fwah grah')

Of all foods, this is possibly the cruelest:

- This well known French delicacy translates as 'fatty liver' because that's exactly what it is. It's also called Strasbourg Pie, due to that European city being a major producer of this very controversial food.

- Foie gras is produced by force-feeding ducks or geese. This is done by workers who shove metal pipes containing grain or fat down the birds' throats. This is carried out as many as three times a day, until the birds' livers bloat. Their livers can end up as much as ten times their normal size.

" *It is the greatest of all mistakes to do nothing because you can only do little. Do what you can.* **"**

Sydney Smith, clergyman (1771- 1845)

- The birds are kept in cramped, tiny cages or in sheds. They have difficulty standing because of their enlarged livers and often peck their own feathers out through stress or start to eat other birds. They are also in constant pain.

- PETA, the Humane Society of the United States, the Animal Defense League, the RSPCA, and the ASPCA have all made very vocal objections to Foie gras.

According to PETA, an investigation they carried out at Hudson Valley Foie Gras in New York (then called Commonwealth Enterprises), found that so many ducks died when their organs ruptured from overfeeding, workers who killed fewer than 50 birds per month were given a bonus.

fact
The force-feeding of birds has been banned in the UK, Turkey, Argentina, Austria, Germany, the Czech Republic, Finland, Italy, Luxembourg, the Netherlands, Norway, Poland, South Africa, Sweden, Switzerland, Denmark, and Israel. However, the sale of this delicacy has not. Despite the UK ban, the country is one of the biggest consumers of the product.

tip
Foie gras may also be labeled as duck or goose pate.

fact
Foie gras is still made in France (where they consider it part of their gastronomical heritage), Bulgaria, Spain and Canada (who are one of the major producers).

" As Foie gras production is too violent to show on an ad, surely this 'torture in a tin' is too violently produced for Selfridges to sell. "

Sir Roger Moore, 2009, quoted in the Daily Telegraph (UK)

In 2009, in the UK, former James Bond star, Sir Roger Moore, both paid and fronted an ad in conjunction with PETA to get department store Selfridges to stop selling Foie gras. There had been plans to show undercover footage of a goose being force-fed, but that was deemed too offensive.

FUR

Most people are in no doubt that fur is cruel. Maybe that's why, in recent years, the fur industry has experienced something of a worldwide decline, although fashion designers, like John Paul Gaultier (in 2008 during Paris Fashion Week, he paraded models down the catwalk wearing real fox heads, as well as clothes made out of fur), continue to design garments using fur.

fact

Stella McCartney, Calvin Klein and Benjamin Cho all refuse to use fur in their designs. They are not alone and its become trendy to go fur free.

Many different animals are killed for their fur. This includes: foxes, rabbits, beavers, Chinchillas, minks, seals, raccoons, bears and, you may be horrified to know this, dogs and cats.

fact

In the case of bears, hundreds of these animals are killed in Canada for the British Ministry of Defence, who use their fur for the famous bearskin hats the Queen's Royal Guards wear. An entire bearskin is needed to make just one hat. The Ministry of Defence claims to have looked at 'ethical alternatives.' Animal rights groups claim they didn't look hard enough.

The UK isn't alone in using bearskins in military hats. Many other army regiments, usually with ceremonial duties, also wear bearskins.

The UK banned fur farming in 2000. Prior to the ban, there were eleven fur farms in the country.

Makeup brushes and applicators may be made out of animal hair or fur. The most commonly used are horse and squirrel hair (both animals are killed) and mink, badger and sable fur. Mink and sable brushes are cruel by-products of the fur industry.

Companies, like Aveda and Urban Decay, use synthetic brushes. Not only are they kinder to animals, they are also kinder to your face as animal brushes are known to cause skin irritation.

HOW DO ANIMALS DIE FOR FUR?

Animals die in a number of ways. The bulk of them in fur farms.

There are no federal humane slaughter laws protecting animals on fur factory farms in America.

Killing methods include:

1. Being caught in steel traps. These animals can suffer in them for days before they are killed and skinned.

2. Animals on fur farms are packed into cramped cages and given meat considered unfit for human consumption. When they get their winter coats, they are killed by electrocution (by having an electrode placed in their bottoms – to make sure the coat is not damaged.) Often this doesn't work the first time.

3. Factory farmed animals can also be gassed to death, have their necks broken or be injected with poison. Many are alive when they are skinned.

4. The Canadians slaughter seals, including baby seals, by shooting or clubbing them to death. Often hakapicks are used. They are clubs with metal hooks on the end. Dying seals are dragged along.

fact

America banned the sale of seal fur in 1972.

fact

In 2009, the EU voted to end the sale of all seal products.

THE CHINESE FUR INDUSTRY

According to PETA, more than half of the fur imported into America comes from China, where fur production is largely unregulated. Animal welfare does not feature. Farmers are allowed to kill animals and treat them in any way they want.

In 2009, an undercover investigation carried out by Swiss Animal Protection/EAST International found that animal cruelty was the norm on fur farms. Farmers kept animals in wired cages, usually where they were exposed to the elements, and animals were beaten and mistreated. Some mothers were so distressed, they killed their own babies.

When the animals are killed for their pelts, it's done by hand and they can be swung and hit against the ground. Often they don't die, are merely stunned, and are then skinned alive.

Cats and dogs are used in the Chinese fur trade. Although cat and dog fur is banned in America, it still manages to get into the country.

fact

People in the UK were shocked to discover that garments they were buying, such as jackets, boots and gloves, made no mention of them containing the fur of cats and dogs. Thanks to a high profile campaign backed by

Paul McCartney and then wife Heather Mills (25,000 signatures were collected in just one online petition), cat and dog fur imports were banned in the EU in 2008.

fact

The EU (the European Union includes the UK, Ireland and France) fur ban was thanks to the tireless work of Member of the European parliament Struan Stevenson, who discovered the booming trade in cat and dog fur. An estimated one million of these animals were slaughtered in China alone, to justify the demand for fur. In 2009, the ban came in and covered all 27 countries in the EU.

fact

The biggest importer of Chinese fur from cats and dogs is now Russia.

HOW DO YOU KNOW WHERE FUR IS PRODUCED?

You don't. Items with fur may be labeled as coming from one country, but this may not be the country where the animal it came from was farmed. Most fur now comes from China because labor costs are so low, so companies make a larger profit.

You also may not know what animal the fur comes from. Whether it's from a fox, a dog, a cat or a rabbit.

fact

There have been many cases where real fur has been passed off and sold as faux fur. In 2010, The *Humane Society of the United States* conducted lab testing and found that a Phillip Lim brand parka, sold online through Barneys New York as 'faux fur,' was, in fact, real animal fur. The same Phillip Lim parka was sold in the Manhattan flagship store without the 'real fur' label required by New York state law.

" Slaughter of these animals is horrific, with cats strangled outside their cages as other cats look on and dogs noosed with metal wires and then slashed across the groin until they bleed to death as the wire noose cuts into their throat. "

European politician Struan Stevenson, speaking after the ban on cat and dog fur in the EU

Source – The Fur Free Alliance. The FFA are an international coalition of over 35 animal protection organizations working to bring an end to the exploitation and killing of animals for their fur. For further information, visit: www.infurmation.com

Please be warned that there may be disturbing images on the website.

HOW DO I KNOW ITS FAUX FUR AND NOT REAL?

In California, in 2010, a law was passed making the labeling of fur garments compulsory in that state. The same law existed in six other states, including New York, Delaware and New Jersey.

Under federal law in America, most fur garments must be labeled, but there is a loophole when it comes to some items, like coats that have fur trims.

It was this loophole that led to *The Truth in Fur Labeling Act of 2010*, which came into affect on March 18th, 2011. *The Humane Society of the United States* heralded the move because now all fur sold in the US, regardless of price, must be labeled as fur. Prior to this, fur garments under the price of $150 did not have to be labeled as fur.

Note – Under the new law, fur items brought in by retailers before March 18th, 2011 did NOT have to be labeled as real fur, although it was suggested that shops voluntarily label them as fur.

IS IT REAL FUR?

The problem of real fur being labeled as fake fur is so bad, animal charities have advised people on how to tell the difference. They stress that you can't tell just by look or touch. Fur can be dyed and shaved to change its appearance and feel. As a result of the demise of the market for fur, there are companies trying to pass real fur off as fake.

The best test, apparently, is the burn test (not very helpful if you want to check it out before you buy). However, this test can tell you whether you've been misled into buying real fur. To do this, cut or pull out some hairs from

" With more than one million items of clothing or accessories being sold with animal fur in the U.S. each year, it only makes sense that consumers know what kind of fur they are wearing. There is an assumption out there that if a garment isn't labeled it must be fake – this isn't always the case. People have a right to know if they are buying dog fur or a polyester blend. It shouldn't be a mystery. "

California Assemblywoman, Fiona Ma

the garment. Carefully light the hairs with a lighter or a match. If it smells like your hair when it's caught in a hair dryer, it's fur.

Another test that is meant to be reliable involves a pin. With faux fur, the pin will go right through the base of the garment. With real fur, it won't.

The Coalition to Abolish the Fur Trade offers advice on their website at **www.caft.org.uk**.

Please be warned that there may be disturbing images.

fact

In the UK, Harrods is the only department store that still sells fur, although the production of fur is illegal in the country. This was correct at the time of writing in 2012.

fact

It's not just clothing that can use real fur. Soft toys may also be made out of fur. Usually this is from factory farmed rabbits. In the UK, sleeping cats that looked like the real thing were sold to unwitting customers, who had no idea real fur was used. Cat and dog fur has also been found on similar toys and ornaments.

LOBSTER

Considering that many lobsters are lobbed into boiling pans whilst they are still alive, whilst the others are killed by people wielding knives and slitting them from head to tail, it's not difficult to see how eating them is considered cruel. Those who defend the practice of boiling claim that the crustaceans don't have a central nervous system and that means they can feel no pain. If you watch a lobster in a boiling pan, you will see it throwing its body around, trying to escape.

In the journal Science, researcher Gordon Gunter described this method of killing lobsters as 'unnecessary torture.'

Whilst lobsters are in tanks waiting to be bought, the people selling them won't feed them. This is to stop the tank filling with ammonia from lobster excrement, as too much can kill lobsters and cooks want them to be fresh. Because they are not fed, these creatures can starve to death, or, in desperation, try to eat each other.

fact

Lobsters carry their young for nine months, like humans do, and can also live to one hundred. Scientists have also determined that they can feel pain.

fact

Lobsters are caught and taken away from their natural habitat and then stored in freezing conditions in a semi-conscious state before they are killed. When they are boiled alive, it can take up to seven minutes for them to die.

MEDICINES

Unfortunately, in most cases, laws insist that all medicines must be tested on animals before they are used on humans, in order for companies to be given licenses to sell them. Scientists argue that this is necessary to make sure the medicines are safe, but the truth is that it's only through testing on humans that you can tell how safe these medicines are. No animal is genetically the same as a human being.

There are many cases where medicines were tested on animals and appeared to be safe and then turned out to be very dangerous to humans. Take Thalidomide for instance. Developed as an anti-sickness drug for pregnant women, Thalidomide had disastrous consequences for many of the people who took it.

Babies were born with deformities, many with missing limbs, as Thalidomide damaged the fetuses in the womb. Other women tragically miscarried. As a result of these tragedies, the drug was banned in the 1960's. Yet animal tests didn't have the same results.

" Why are we appalled by the cruelty companion animals suffer, yet we ignore the suffering of lab animals? Do they not deserve the same protections? "

Anon

fact

There are testing methods that do NOT involve using animals, which are more reliable then animal testing and will hopefully one day replace all animal testing, including human skin cells created in a test tube.

fact

When it comes to prescription drugs, Beagles are one of the most experimented on animals. Drugs for cancer, heart disease, heart attacks and infectious diseases are tested on Beagles, who are used because of their gentle, friendly nature and desire to please. Some of the tests conducted on them are considered barbaric by many.

One test involves them being forced to inhale chemicals by having a gas mask type device forcibly latched onto their noses and faces. They also have substances dripped into their eyes, have tubes inserted into their stomachs to force-feed them and are restrained whilst they have substances pumped directly into their bloodstreams.

In most cases, anesthetic is not used and these dogs suffer in agony.

In many cases, these tests have been done countless times before in other countries.

fact

One of the reasons why animal tests are not reliable is that diseases are artificially induced. A disease that is generated is not the same as a disease that someone has developed, often over time, through their environment or diet.

tip

If you want to end the testing of medicines on animals, then back the charities that are looking to replace animal experiments. This includes organizations like the British Union for the Abolition of Vivisection (The BUAV) who are leading the way.

For more details, visit the following organizations' websites:

www.buav.org and click on 'Humane science.'

The National Anti-Vivisection Society at **www.navs.org.uk**

Animal Defenders International are a global organization who also campaign to replace animal experiments. **www.ad-international.org**

The Dr Hadwen Trust for Humane Research (DHT) offers grants to scientists in the UK to carry out non-animal experiments. **www.drhadwentrust.org**

tip

Give money to charities that commission non-animal research for conditions like cancer and Alzheimer's. Experts say that the many years and the millions that have been spent using animals to find cures, by conducting experiments, are wasteful and have not advanced medical science.

To read more about charities that don't fund animal testing on their behalf and those that do, go to **www.peta.org/living/beauty-and-personal-care/naughty-nice-charities.aspx**

The Physicians Committee for Responsible Medicine (PCRM) has a searchable database of charities that don't fund animal research at **www.humaneseal.org/search.cfm**

You can search for charities in the USA, Canada, the UK and Australia. Charities awarded their 'Humane Charity Seal of Approval' are those that are committed to advancing medical research without using animals.

In the UK, Animal Aid has a list of charities that only commission non-animal medical research. **www.animalaid.org.uk/h/n/CAMPAIGNS/experiments/ALL/281**

Note – the list is constantly updated and the policies of some charities may change.

fact

Despite the many millions poured into animal research, an effective animal model (one that is truly representative of a human being) hasn't yet been identified for HIV. This is no surprise, as HIV stands for Human Immunodeficiency Virus. This means HIV is specifically a human virus. Animals can't contract it.

MEGA DAIRIES

One thing that could also have been added to this list of things that can never be cruelty free, is milk produced by cows in mega dairies. These cows are kept inside crowded and dimly lit sheds or warehouses for the majority of their lives and these dairies have a 'zero grazing' system (the cows are never put out to pastures in fields). This has been linked to health problems in the cows that people fear could be passed onto humans through the cows' milk.

Cows in mega dairies have a greater chance of infection, caused by living in such closed, crowded quarters and never being out in the fresh air.

These types of farms are common in America and there is a move to have them throughout Europe.

fact

In 2011, a campaign led by animal rights organizations and Compassion in World Farming (set up by dairy farmer Peter Roberts in 1967), managed to get a plan by Nocton Dairies withdrawn. Nocton wanted to build what would have been the first mega dairy in Western Europe, in Lincolnshire in the UK. It would have housed almost 4,000 cows. Over 72,000 people signed a petition opposing the plan, including local residents.

It's up to you to decide whether you think drinking milk produced by mega dairies is supporting a cruel trade or not.

" What good does it do you to test something (a vaccine) in a monkey? You find five or six years from now that it works in the monkey, and then you test it in humans and you realize that humans behave totally differently from monkeys, so you've wasted five years. "

Dr. Mark Feinberg, a leading AIDS researcher

fact

No milk is produced without cruelty. Mothers have their young taken away so the milk they produce for their children can be used by humans. Often the male baby calves are killed to be eaten or put in veal crates. The mothers are often pumped full of steroids so that they will produce more milk than nature intended to meet the huge demand for milk in the West.

fact

Milk has been linked with breast cancer. In China, where they don't consume milk products, their rate of breast cancer amongst women is a fraction of what it is in the West, where dairy is part of people's everyday diet. According to Cancer Research UK, the risk of a woman getting breast cancer in her life is one in eight. In the USA, the rate is similar.

tip

Try soy (Soya) milk, rice or oat milk. They are much better for you and can help reduce cholesterol.

SHEEPSKIN

Unlike wool, in the case of sheepskin, the sheep does have to be killed first:

- As its name suggests, sheepskin, is more than just wool. In fact, it's the equivalent of wearing fur because the wool is still attached to the skin when it's taken off. Hence the word sheepskin.

- Ugg boots are made from sheepskin and so are many pieces of footwear, like slippers, as well as other things, like coats and jackets. It will say sheepskin on the label, as it's in a shop's best interest to state this because it makes the item worth more.

- Faux sheepskin can be just as warm as the real thing and is readily available at a much lower cost than real sheepskin – so it's better for your pocket as well as for the sheep.

You have to decide whether to wear sheepskin or not. The main argument for wearing sheepskin is the same as for wearing leather – that the animal was dead anyway, because sheepskin comes from lambs and sheep killed to be eaten. The makers of Uggs say that no animal cruelty is involved because sheepskin is a natural by-product of the food industry.

The main argument against this is that an animal was killed for the sheepskin; therefore its production was far from cruelty free.

fact

Pamela Anderson blamed herself for starting the craze for Ugg boots when she was on Baywatch because she used to wear them with her famous red swimsuit.

fact

It's not just sheepskin that involves cruelty. Australia produces most of the world's merino wool. Many farmers there use a process called 'mulesing' which means a device that looks like garden shears is used to cut huge chunks of skin and flesh away from merino lambs so that the animals won't get something called fly strike, which can kill them. Farmers have a choice to breed fly strike resistant sheep, but choose not to do this.

fact

You can buy boots that look like Ugg boots at a fraction of the cost, which don't contain sheepskin. These days, synthetic fabrics are of a good quality. Usually they are labeled as containing sheepskin (as it justifies the high cost of the finished product), but not always.

tip

Sheepskin can also sneak its way into furniture, like sofas, chairs, cushions as well as bedding, handbags and children's clothing. And, believe it or not, shampoo.

" I used to wear them with my red swimsuit to keep warm – never realizing that they were skin! Do not buy UGGs! Buy Stella McCartney or Juicy boots. "

Pamela Anderson

VEAL

Veal has a delicate taste and texture, which is why it's considered such a delicacy. Mention the word and, although people may have tried it, they are probably unaware of how it is made.

Veal is basically made from the meat of male baby calves. These calves are taken away from their mothers, sometimes when they are no more than a few hours old, but usually when they are days old. They will never see their mothers again. They are placed in wooden crates so small they are unable to turn around, never mind walk and they are deprived of any light and human contact. Some calves are chained by their necks to stop them moving at all. They are fed mainly on a milk diet. This is to ensure that their meat is pale in color. Many become anemic (anaemic) because of their restrictive diet and lack of sunlight.

After four to five months, they are transported to the slaughterhouse in trucks, where they are killed to produce what is described as 'milk-fed veal.' By this stage, most of the calves are unable to walk.

Not all veal calves suffer this fate. Some are killed within hours or days of being born, to be used as low grade veal, which is often called 'bob' veal.

Although not used as veal, the female calves are often taken away from their mothers, too. They are put in small huts until they are old enough to have calves themselves and produce milk.

fact

When cows have their calves taken away from them, they react by bellowing and get into a distressed state, just like human mothers would if they were forcibly separated from their babies.

Going
Free-range
& Cage-free

II Choosing free-range eggs and reading food labels, to ensure you buy processed products containing free-range eggs, can make a big difference to the quality of life for hens. II

Jane Howorth, Chief Executive of the British Hen Welfare Trust.

Chapter 3
Going Free-range & Cage-free

The attitude of consumers is changing – at least in the UK. Where once it seemed no one cared about the eggs they fried in the morning coming from battery hens, free-range sales outstripped caged hen eggs for the first time in 2008 in the UK, according to the British Egg Information Service.

This is because of all the publicity about battery hens and the miserable existence they endure to meet the UK's egg needs.

Most UK supermarkets also only use free-range eggs in their own brand products and some stores, like Marks & Spencer's, Waitrose, Sainsbury's and Morrisons, have stopped selling eggs from caged hens altogether. This is due to declining demand and the need to be seen as more ethical.

The change in shopping habits has shown that British consumers value compassion for animals over cost, as free-range eggs are more expensive than ones produced by battery hens. Free-range eggs tend to cost more money and ones produced where the hens have been fed on high quality grain (many hens are fed chicken meal, which is basically dead hens) are even more expensive.

THE BRITISH HEN TRUST

In the UK, hens have their own charity to look out for their welfare. The British Hen Welfare Trust (formerly known as The Battery Hen Trust) not only re-homes battery hens, they also try and educate the public about hen welfare. For more details, visit their site at www.bhwt.org.uk. The charity has a number of celebrity supporters, including chef Jamie Oliver.

In 2010, the charity celebrated finding a home for their 200th bird. Fittingly enough for a moment that required the popping of some champagne corks, the hen was called Fizz.

UNITED STATES AND CANADA

Sadly, in the USA and Canada things are very different. The majority of eggs are from caged hens, and the criteria for eggs to be described as free-range are different to those in the UK and are nowhere near as strict. However, this could be changing in America.

In 2011, work by Farm Sanctuary and the Humane Society of the United States activists in California, Ohio, Washington, and Oregon has brought the United Egg Producers to the table. They agreed to aggressively support federal legislation that would lessen the suffering of 280 million laying hens.

The legislation would mean:

- The eventual phasing out of the existing battery cages, which are so small hens can't stretch out one wing never mind two.

- The introduction of cages that would offer hens twice the space they currently have.

- Egg producers offering what are called 'environment enrichments' for hens. This could include perching posts, nesting boxes and scratching areas.

- Making it mandatory to put labeling on the box of eggs saying exactly how they were produced. Say 'eggs from cage free hens' and 'eggs from caged hens' so that shoppers can make an informed choice.

- Improving the standards of euthanasia (the way hens are killed, including baby chicks).

- Cutting down on the amount of Ammonia in the hens' environment; something which, in excessive amounts, is dangerous to both the humans who work in henhouses and to the birds.

- Stopping the practice of starving birds to make them molt. This is used to interfere with the laying process.

- Restricting the sale of egg and egg products that fail to meet those standards.

Note – Although better for the hens, these improvements don't mean hens are free-range, i.e. allowed out in the open.

fact

By January 2012, battery cages will be banned across the EU (the European Union, which includes the UK, Ireland and France). The new colony cages provide a third more of the space currently legally required by each bird, along with a nest, perching space and a scratching area. Animal welfare charities claim these 'enriched' cages still do not give the birds enough space and are still battery cages. Birds will never get to see the sun or indulge in natural behaviors. Hens are very sociable animals.

In America, the future is bleaker for battery hens because 95% of eggs sold come from factory farmed birds, although, as previously mentioned, the conditions they are forced to live in could improve in the future, but not sufficiently for most people in animal welfare.

BATTERY HENS

So, what's all the fuss about? Is the battery hen industry cruel?

Judge for yourself by the following facts, which refer to hens in the UK (in countries like America, the conditions hens live in are much worse):

" For too long, animals on factory farms have had no federal protection from even the most heinous abuse. This new federal bill would ensure modest yet historic improvements for egg-laying hens, and we encourage Washingtonians to urge their lawmakers to enact it as soon as possible. "

Gene Baur, president and co-founder of Farm Sanctuary

- All hens are in cages, sometimes with up to four other birds. There isn't enough room for them to turn around.

- Legal requirements mean each given bird is given just under three quarters the size of an A4 sheet of paper in the UK.

- The cages are usually in large sheds, with one cage packed on top of another.

- These hens are kept indoors and never see sunlight. Any light they get is artificial.

- They all have to be de-beaked (have their beaks trimmed) to prevent them attacking each other, themselves or workers, because of the stress of confinement. De-beaking is done when the birds are as young as one day old and then again at about seven weeks old. A hot machine blade is often used and the process is painful. It has been likened to humans having their hands chopped off.

- Many birds die because of diseases they get caused by having to sit in their own poop.

- Once they stop laying eggs, they are killed for pet food.

- Rescued battery hens can hardly walk, are scared of the outdoors and need to have their long nails clipped.

fact

In Australia, it's estimated that more than 95% of all hens have had their beaks trimmed and that includes on free-range farms. In Switzerland, Sweden and Austria, hens rarely have their beaks trimmed.

fact

In 2010, the UK government backed out of a ban on de-beaking that was to come into force in 2011. The Farm Animal Welfare Council (FAW) still insists they want an eventual ban on the practice. Compassion in World Farming (CiWF) also backed the ban.

The Welfare of Laying Hens Directive stipulates that for eggs to be termed 'free-range', hens must have continuous daytime access to runs that are mainly covered with vegetation and with a maximum stocking density of 2,500 birds per hectare.
Source – British Egg Industry Council

In America, it's a different story.

FREE-RANGE EGGS IN AMERICA

In America, USDA regulations apply only to poultry (birds like hens) and indicate that animals have been allowed to go outside. The USDA regulations, however, do not specify the quality or size of the outside area, or the amount of time the animal must spend outside or be able to go outside. Hens can spend as little as five minutes outside and still have their eggs labeled as free-range. In the UK, this wouldn't be allowed, but there was one case where caged eggs were passed off as free-range so the seller could make more money.

tip

In America, free-range is often confused with 'yarding' where hens are kept fenced in yards, but this is not the same as free-range.

fact

Most hens in America have their beaks trimmed or are de-beaked, which is the same thing.

FREE-RANGE EGGS IN CANADA

In Canada, free-range eggs come from hens and chickens who are allowed to roam freely outside. These eggs will have the Animal Welfare Approved Eggs label.

Labels on eggs that are not free-range often say things like 'farm fresh' and 'all natural' making you think of hens running free, when they're actually in cages or sheds. Other misleading terms include 'cage free' or 'free run.' This means that hens may be allowed to roam freely inside the sheds where they are housed, but there isn't much room to do so and some hens end up cannibalizing (eating) their fellow kind out of frustration, boredom or hunger.

`fact`

Most eggs sold in Canada are from battery hens.

`fact`

Canadian free-range egg producers do not have to have their products certified unless they also claim they are organic. This means anyone can label their eggs free-range.

Eggs may even be called free-range when the hen that laid them has to go in a cage or back in a shed. Nor does the label guarantee that the bird has been fed healthy food.

FREE RANGE EGGS IN AUSTRALIA

In Australia, 80% of eggs are from caged birds. Considering that it's a country full of wide, open spaces, that may come as a shock.

There is NO legal, enforceable legislation for the standards of free-range eggs in Australia. This means that it's very easy for egg producers to label their eggs free-range.

There's also a difference in standards, this usually involves the amount of time they are allowed outside, whether they are given growth promoters (steroids) and whether they have their beaks trimmed or not.

`tip`

If you want to ensure your eggs are truly free range, the only way to do it is to get your own laying hens.

" *God loved the birds and invented trees. Man loved the birds and invented cages.* **"**

Jacques Deval

FREE-RANGE EGGS IN THE UK

In the UK, free-range hens have access to the outdoors and are not confined in cages.

The UK has the strongest legislation for free-range eggs in the world.

Note – eggs from 'free run' hens in the UK, are not to be confused with free-range. Free run simply means they have free run of their environment, which is a dark shed in most cases. These hens don't usually have access to the outdoors and natural sunlight.

IS FREE-RANGE THE SAME AS ORGANIC?

There are a number of differences between free-range and organic egg systems in the UK, which explains why organic, free-range eggs are that much more expensive:

- Free-range hens are almost always de-beaked, organic hens are not.

- Organic hens are not given genetically modified food. Free-range hens can be.

- Organic hens are not given antibiotics, but free-range ones usually are.

- Organic hens are not fed with any animal by-products, like dead hens, free-range hens can be.

- Free-range hens can be kept in cramped conditions, organic ones roam free.

- Organic hens are not given feed that has been treated with pesticides or have added colorants. Organic means no chemicals are used.

Note – Don't assume all organic eggs come from free-range egg systems.

WHAT ARE BARN EGGS?

Barn hens are kept in large windowless sheds. They have perches and bedding and are free to roam in the sheds, but they aren't usually allowed to go outside.

WHAT DO THE CODES ON UK EGGS MEAN?

In the UK, eggs must be coded by law. Eggs are routinely checked using ultraviolet lights that show up the wire marks that are on battery hen eggs.

The first number refers to the farming method.

0 – organic

1 – Free-range

2 – Barn

3 – Cage

This is followed by the country of origin and the farm ID, which tells you exactly where these eggs came from.

IS THERE AN EGG CODING SYSTEM IN AMERICA?

No, in America, there is no coding system for eggs. Phrases like 'free roaming' and 'all natural' are often used. This also does not mean products are free-range. The only word on labels regulated by the US government is 'organic.'

ARE FREE-RANGE EGGS BETTER FOR ME, AND IF SO WHY?

Professor Michael Crawford, of the institute of brain chemistry and human nutrition at London Metropolitan University, found that free-range hens produce more nutritious eggs.

This is no surprise, as, unlike their caged friends, they are not left in diseased ridden cages to lie in their own mess and to peck away at the birds sharing those cages because of the stress.

WHY DO FREE-RANGE EGGS COST MORE?

Battery hens produce more eggs, because there are much more of them cramped into a confined space. Free-range hens and chickens also cost more to feed because they are generally fed better than factory hens. In the UK, they also must have access to the open air. This means egg producers need more land.

Note that, in America, the rules on free-range hens and chickens are much laxer. Having as little as five minutes in the outdoors is considered sufficient to describe their eggs as free-range.

In Canada, free-range means the same as it does in the UK, i.e. hens that are allowed to run about outside.

WHY DO SOME PEOPLE STILL SAY FREE-RANGE EGGS ARE CRUEL?

Egg producers have no use for male chicks, so they're killed by crushing or gassing. Many are fed in handfuls and dropped alive into a mincing machine in a process known as IMD – Instantaneous Mechanical Destruction. This was shown in undercover footage by Viva! (Vegetarians International Voice for Animals) in the UK when they filmed at a hatchery.

Both of these methods are approved by the UK Government's food and farming department, Defra, and the Humane Slaughter Association. Yet if you did that to a pet bird, you would be prosecuted.

fact

Most people say they are against factory farming, but 80 percent of meat comes from factory farming.
Source – Viva!

" Who can believe that there is no soul behind those luminous eyes! "*

Theophile Gautier

Going Vegetarian or Vegan

" If slaughterhouses had glass walls, everyone would be vegetarian. "

Sir Paul McCartney

Chapter 4
Going Vegetarian or Vegan

One of the best ways to live a cruelty free life is by going vegetarian, because by doing that you're not contributing to the number of animals being killed for meat and products containing slaughterhouse by-products like gelatin (gelatine).

You could go even further and go vegan to avoid all animal products, like leather, wool, eggs, milk and honey.

In 2008, American magazine, Vegetarian Times, conducted a 'Vegetarianism in America' study, which found some interesting facts:

- 7.3million Americans are vegetarian.

- 22.8million live a 'vegetarian inclined' lifestyle. This means they were actively trying to eat less meat. People who do this are often referred to as meat reducers.

In the UK, there are is an estimated 4million people who are vegetarian. Around 5 percent of that number are vegans who consume and use no animal products at all.

VEGETARIANS

There are different types of vegetarians, although most vegetarians will simply call themselves vegetarian and say whether they eat eggs and drink milk.

ALL vegetarians abstain from eating meat and that includes fish and fowl. This is usually because they disagree with killing animals for food when there is so much more cruelty free food available. Most vegetarians will not wear items that are made from killed animals and this includes leather and fur.

- Lacto-Vegetarians (also called lactarians) don't eat animal flesh (meat) and that includes fish and poultry (chicken, turkey, etc). They do drink milk and eat products containing milk. But they don't eat eggs. This is the most common type of vegetarian in India, where the majority of the world's vegetarians live. Most vegetarians there are Hindus.

- Ovo-lacto Vegetarians don't eat meat, including poultry and fish. However, they do consume dairy and egg products (usually only free-range eggs). This is the most common type of vegetarian in the US, UK, Canada and Australia.

fact
Before the word vegetarian was coined around 1840, the term used was 'vegetable diet.' Some people referred to themselves as Pythagoreans after the ancient Greek Pythagoras (570c-495BC) who set up a school in Italy. Pythagoras believed in the transmigration of the soul (reincarnation) and because of that, his followers were vegetarian. He also believed that men and women were equal, an unusual belief at that time.

VEGANS

The word vegan was invented by founder of *The Vegan Society*, Donald Watson, in the 1940's. World Vegan Day, the date of the society's founding, November 1, is now celebrated every year.

Although vegans are a type of vegetarian, they are not to be confused with vegetarians as they do not eat or use any animal products at all. This includes eating or using products that don't involve the death of animals and cruelty, like consuming honey or wearing wool. Vegans don't use leather either.

❝ I was surrounded by interesting animals. They all 'gave' something: the farm horse pulled the plough, the lighter horse pulled the trap, the cows 'gave' milk, the hens 'gave' eggs and the cockerel was a useful 'alarm clock' – I didn't realise at that time that he had another function too. The sheep 'gave' wool. I could never understand what the pigs 'gave', but they seemed such friendly creatures – always glad to see me. **❞**

Donald Watson, inventor of the word vegan, explaining his decision to become vegan. It was realizing what the 'pigs gave' at the age of 14 that made him turn vegetarian

It can be very tricky being a vegan as many products that appear vegan are not. For instance, some breakfast cereals have vitamin D added that comes from sheep's wool, and the majority of condoms contain milk proteins, so are not considered vegan. There are vegan condoms that exist, which use cocoa powder. Candy (sweets) may also be glazed with beeswax, which vegans don't eat.

WHY PEOPLE GO VEGAN/VEGETARIAN

- For animal welfare reasons – They don't want to eat animals. Perhaps they think the way animals are farmed and killed is wrong, or they simply think it's immoral to kill another living thing to eat when there are so many other things humans can eat instead.

- For lifestyle beliefs – They don't think it's morally wrong to eat animals, they just think it's healthier and is less likely to make them put on weight. This type of vegetarian is in the minority.

- For religious reasons – Some sects of Hinduism are vegetarian. Followers of the Jainism religion believe that all sentient beings are equal and don't eat animals. About half of all Buddhists are vegetarian. Some Sikhs also believe it's wrong to eat meat.

- For health reasons – Going veggie is meant to help with a variety of conditions, including heart disease, high cholesterol, type 2 diabetes, osteoporosis, arthritis, allergies, asthma, environmental illness, hypertension, gout, gallstones, hemorrhoids, kidney stones, ulcers, colitis, premenstrual syndrome, anxiety, and depression. The list is a very long one.

- Being vegetarian also reduces your risk of getting many different types of cancer and heart disease. Vegetarians are also less likely to be obese.

fact

India has the most vegetarians of any country in the world. An estimated 40 percent of its 1.2billion people are vegetarian.

" One day I was helping my mom make dinner, cutting up a chicken, and I hit a tumor with the knife. There was pus and blood all over the place. That was enough for me. **"**

Actor Josh Hartnett

IS IT SAFE FOR CHILDREN TO BE VEGAN OR VEGETARIAN?

The key for everyone is to have a balanced diet containing foods that have all the things your body needs, like protein, vitamins and minerals. This is vital whether you follow a traditional diet of eating meat and animal by-products or have a diet with no animal products.

In the case of a vegetarian diet, it is perfectly safe for children to be on this diet as long as that diet is balanced. However, in the case of vegan children, they may need to take supplements like B12. This is not always the case, as vegan parents tend to be more knowledgeable about nutrition than other parents and cook food from scratch, so they tend to serve up much less processed food with nasty trans fats and e numbers that can cause obesity and hyperactivity in children.

tip

Always seek advice before changing diet, especially a child's. If you are a woman who is vegan or vegetarian, remember that, if you have any deficiencies, your baby's nutritional needs will not be met through breastfeeding. You may have to take supplements if your diet is lacking in certain vitamins and minerals.

Please see '**Vegetarian & Vegan Organizations**' at the back of book for details of organizations where you can seek advice.

HOW ANIMALS ARE KILLED FOR FOOD

In America

The Humane Slaughter Act (also known as the Humane Methods of Livestock Slaughter Act), is a federal law passed in 1958 that is supposed to protect animals during their slaughter. In reality, it is a weak act.

Under the act, animals must be unconscious when they are killed. This is done by stunning. The Act does not cover fish and birds, such as hens, chickens, ducks and turkeys. This is seen as surprising by animal welfare groups as Americans consume a lot of poultry.

The Act has been criticized for a number of reasons:

- Not being enforced properly by the United States Department of Agriculture (USDA). Inspectors claim they cannot enforce the law because they continually have difficulty getting into slaughterhouses.

- Slaughterhouses are accused of breaching the law and not being penalized for it. The Washington Post reported that, in 1998, a Texas beef company cited 22 times for chopping the hooves off cattle, whilst the animals were still alive, escaped any punishment.

- Having no power. Under the revised act of 1978, inspectors were allowed to stop the slaughter line if they saw the act being flouted. They could do little else.

- Not covering all animals killed for meat. Under this law, there is no requirement for how birds should be killed.

- Not covering the welfare of the animals in the months or years up to their deaths.

- Being out of date and not reflecting modern standards of animal welfare and more compassionate practices.

fact

Hens, chickens and ducks are placed head first on a conveyor belt whilst fully conscious, and have their necks cut by a mechanical cutter. If the cutter works, they bleed to death. If it doesn't work, they are alive when they are immersed in scalding water so their feathers will come off.

fact

Cattle are stunned with a captive bolt gun and then have their throats cut. They bleed to death, usually whilst shackled and hung upside down. Sometimes they are killed with electricity.

The UK

Most animals in the UK are stunned with a captive bolt pistol before they are killed because all animals must be stunned before they are slaughtered in the UK (see below for religious exemptions to the law). This is meant to make them unconscious so they feel no pain but there is no proof this is the case. Sometimes the stunning doesn't work, and either has to be done again or no one notices because animals are killed in an assembly line.

Once stunned, animals are shackled by a hind leg and hoisted above the ground. A slaughter man then cuts the animal's throat, using a very sharp knife. This severs the major blood vessels in the animal's neck and chest, which supply the brain, and ensures rapid blood loss. The animals bleed to death. Meat not produced in this way is not considered to be saleable.

Chickens are lifted by their heads until they are immersed in electrified water baths so they can be electrically stunned and become unconscious, but many try to get free and the stunning fails. Chickens and pigs are put in scalding hot water to get rid of their hair and feathers. Sometimes they are still conscious when this happens.

Chickens are usually killed by a mechanical cutter in an assembly line to speed up the process. This is done when they are hanging upside down by their legs on metal shackles on a moving conveyor belt. Chickens can also be gassed to death, as can hens and turkeys.

Religious exemptions to the UK law

There are religious exceptions to the UK law on stunning that makes it compulsory to stun all animals before they are killed for food:

- Animals intended to be eaten by Muslims and Jews don't have to be stunned first.

- It used to be the case that animals destined to be halal meat weren't stunned first, but that has changed and an estimated 90% of animals are stunned.

- In order for meat to be considered halal (for Muslims) and Shechita (for Jews) the exposed necks of animals are cut with a sharp knife.

- The ritual slaughter of animals with a knife is justified on religious grounds (Muslims are not allowed to consume blood or 'dead meat', and claim pre-stunning will prevent the entire animal's blood from draining away) and on the assertion that the animal becomes unconscious immediately and feels no pain. Footage of ritual slaughter taken by PETA found that animals were in pain and took as long as three minutes to die.

- For meat to be suitable for followers of Judaism, the animals can't be stunned first as the animal must be healthy before Jews can eat it. But, a pre-cut stun is becoming more commonplace – only in the case of cows and sheep, but not for birds. This means the animals are stunned and they have their throats cut right away.

- Animals that are not stunned are fully conscious as they bleed out and are fully aware of their surroundings.

fact

Under European law, meat that is halal or Kosher must be labeled. This is to allow consumers to decide whether they want to eat it or not.

In the UK, there was public outrage when it emerged that people had unwittingly eaten halal meat when they dined out, ate at public events and bought meat from the supermarket. People were angry because they weren't made aware of this and weren't given the choice of whether to eat the meat or not.

VEGETARIANS & FOOD LABELING

In America and the UK, foods tend to be labeled as being suitable for vegetarians or vegans. In other countries, like Australia and Germany, people are not so lucky. Knowing what to eat can mean scouring the list of ingredients (see '**Hidden nasties in our food**' later on in this chapter for things to look out for).

tip

Some companies, like Nestle, have 'free from' lists that tell you what products are suitable for vegetarians, vegans and those with allergies. Visit company websites for details. Look for 'suitable for vegetarians list,' 'nutritional information' or 'dietary information.'

America

Under American law, most ingredients must be listed on the label. Meat must be listed if it appears as a stand-alone ingredient, but the problem for vegetarians and vegans is that, under the definition of 'natural flavor,' manufactures can mask a variety of meat derived products. This includes meat derivatives like chicken and fish stock, poultry, seafood and dairy products, which may be used to flavor or bulk up products.

Products may also be labeled as vegan or vegetarian even if they were made in an environment with animal derived products, risking the chance of cross contamination.

Food makers only have to label suitable products as vegan or vegetarian if they want to. They are under no legal obligation to do so.

The Food Ingredient Right to Know Act, which would have made it easier for vegetarians to identify friendly foods, was launched in 2009. Under the proposal, foods would have to name any flavoring, or coloring derived from meat, poultry, or other animal products (including insects) on the label under a new amended Federal Food, Drug and Cosmetic Act. The bill ran out of time.

The American Vegetarian Association has an AVA Certified logo that clearly shows whether products are vegetarian or vegan.

Just because a product carries a 'meat free' label does not mean it's suitable for vegetarians. It may contain slaughterhouse by-products like gelatin or fish.

The UK

There is no legal definition for vegetarian in the UK or the European Union. The Vegetarian Society in the UK wants there to be because, at the moment, foods can carry a 'suitable for vegetarians' or a simple V symbol and contain battery farmed eggs. Most vegetarians only eat free-range eggs.

Note, foods that have the 'Vegetarian Society approved' green V logo (in the UK) are made from free-range eggs. Quorn products also carry this logo. This is the most trusted vegetarian logo.

Stores also have their own suitable for vegetarian labeling on their products, whether it's wording like 'vegetarian,' which usually appears down from the list of ingredients and near where a warning for nut allergy sufferers is printed. Or, it can appear on the front of the packaging as either a V symbol or in word form 'suitable for vegetarians', near the nutritional breakdown, including the amount of calories contained in the product.

Sadly, very few foodstuffs are labeled as being suitable for vegans, even when products are. In those cases, a consumer is faced with two options – not to buy, or to scrutinize the ingredients themselves. Seeing a vegetarian logo at least means there's a chance a product is vegan friendly.

Foods labeled as suitable for vegetarians or vegans are, however, subject to provisions within the Trades Descriptions Act 1968.

In 2006, the Food Standards Agency in the UK (FSA) published guidance aimed at improving food labeling for vegans and vegetarians. The Vegetarian Society and the Vegan Society were consulted, along with other shareholders. For the first time, criteria for the use of terms vegetarian and vegan on food labels was established.

This states the term 'vegetarian' should not be applied to foods that are, or are made from or with the aid of, products derived from animals that have died, have been slaughtered, or animals that die as a result of being eaten. Animals means farmed, wild or domestic animals, including, for example, livestock, poultry, game, fish, shellfish, crustaceans, amphibians, tunicates, echinoderms, mollusks* and insects – Source, Foods Standards Agency (UK) website at **www.food.gov.uk**.

The Food Standards Agency also states – 'The term 'vegan' should not be applied to foods that are, or are made from or with the aid of animals or animal products (including products from living animals).'

In addition, manufacturers, retailers and caterers of products labeled vegetarian or vegan, also have to show that foods labeled in this way have not been contaminated with non-vegetarian or vegan products when they were made, prepared or stored. If there's a chance of this, the label must carry a warning along the lines of 'this was prepared in a factory making meat/fish products.'

fact

The Vegan logo is a registered trademark that shows items that bear it have met 'vegan animal free standards.' Source – The Vegan Society website.

---

* spelt mollusk in America, this refers to over a thousand creatures that have soft bodies, which are usually protected by shells, like shellfish, squids, scallops, snails, mussels, clams, etc.

MYTHS ABOUT VEGETARIANISM

Perhaps the most common one is that vegetarians are skinny and pale looking because they don't get the iron the human body gets from eating meat.

But there are many more things that have high iron contents that don't come from dead animals:

- Sesame seeds have a higher iron count than most meats. They can also be eaten in a variety of ways – on their own, in salads or in bread.

- Cashew nuts are a good source of iron. Ideally with no salt.

- Dried fruits, like apricots, prunes and raisins.

- Beans. Lima beans in particular, have a high iron content.

- Green leafy vegetables, like spinach and lettuce.

- Dark chocolate.

- Whole grains, such as popcorn, brown or wild rice, whole grain breads, quinoa and bulgar wheat.

- Curry powder. High in iron, the only trouble is that we generally don't eat a lot of it.

- In addition, vegetarian friendly iron is added to all breakfast cereals and some bread.

tip

Having something containing vitamin C at the same time as a food with iron helps the body to absorb iron. Avoid having anything that interferes with the body absorbing iron at the same time as you have something with iron. This means no caffeine, no milk and soy (Soya), although it contains an easily absorbed iron; it also contains a substance that can lower the body's iron absorption rate.

IF WE ALL STOPPED EATING MEAT, FARM ANIMALS WOULD DIE OUT

Animals are being bred in their masses for food. If more people decided to stop eating meat, there simply wouldn't be as many animals being bred by man just to be eaten.

EATING MEAT IS MANLY

This goes back to the days when man was the hunter gatherer whilst the women stayed at home. The implication with this view is that choosing to be a compassionate human being somehow dilutes someone's manliness. In response to this, vegetarians and vegans could politely point out that there is nothing vaguely macho about eating a domesticated animal that has been farmed and then killed by someone else for them to eat.

YOU NEED MEAT TO SURVIVE

Millions of vegetarians the world over are proof that this is simply not true. This idea comes from the belief that all humans need protein and you can only get that from meat. Yet protein can come from a number of plant sources like bananas, tofu, soybeans (the richest source of plant protein), seitan[*] (pronounced say- tahn, but also called gluten in America and wheat meat), Quorn (not vegan as it contains eggs), gardein (available in America and Canada only and suitable for vegans) and nuts and seeds.

IT'S NOT HEALTHY FOR CHILDREN TO BE VEGETARIAN

At a time when many children are vastly overweight because of meat laden convenience foods and not eating enough fruit and vegetables, how can a diet that is rich in fruit and vegetables possibly be detrimental to their health? As long as all dietary requirements are met, children who grow up not eating meat are generally healthier than those who eat meat, because they eat so much more of the good stuff.

[*] Seitan is a low fat, high protein meat alternative that comes from the protein part of wheat. It's not suitable for anyone with a gluten intolerance. It has been used for thousands of years in the Middle East, Asia and Russia.

HIDDEN NASTIES IN OUR FOOD

There are ingredients in our food that, at first glance, you would assume were cruelty free, but you'd be wrong –

ANIMAL RENNET

Most vegetarians do eat dairy products like milk and cheese because no animal had to die to produce these two products, but vegans abstain from all animal products, so they don't consume any dairy products.

Not all cheeses are suitable for vegetarians because they may contain animal rennet. There is no such thing as cruelty free animal rennet. It's produced from the stomach lining of killed baby calves. Yet synthetic rennet can be used instead. This is usually used in vegetarian cheese.

Animal rennet may also be present in some potato chips (crisps) and cheese type sauces.

The good news is that most supermarket cheeses in America, Canada and the UK are suitable for vegetarians, but, unless a cheese is labeled as 'vegetarian' or 'suitable for vegetarians' or 'containing/made with vegetable rennet,' it's not vegetarian.

COCHINEAL

This is normally used in foods that need a reddish/pinkish and orange coloring, but is also used in cosmetics. It's made by picking the insects off cacti before killing them in hot water and then drying and pulverizing their bodies.

It can also be down on the label as carmine, Carminic Acid, Carmines Natural Red 4 and E120, which is the name of the dye extracted from the insects' bodies and eggs. Fears over artificial dyes have led to the increased use of this dye, which was first used in 15th century South America, but carmine can cause asthma in some people and hyperactivity in children.

Many Muslims consider carmine-containing food haram (forbidden) because the dye is extracted from insects, and Jewish people also avoid foodstuffs containing this additive.

Cochineal and carmine can be found in meat, poultry, sausages, soft drinks, alcohol, cakes and pastries as a topping, preserves, desserts and sweets.

As of January 5th, 2011, the U.S. Food and Drug Administration regulation requires all foods and cosmetics containing cochineal to declare it on their ingredient labels. This is because of health concerns over the substance.

GELATIN (spelt gelatine in the UK)

This is made by boiling the bones, skin and tendons of animals and is most commonly used in jello (jelly in the UK), marshmallows, jelly type candies (sweets) like Jelly Babies and some low fat yoghurts and desserts. It can also be used in some soft drinks to disperse the color.

Gelatin can be bought in the form of granules, powder and sheets for household use, usually in baking as a gelling agent.

Gelatin's E number is 441 and it's a by-product of the meat and leather industry. It comes mainly from cows and pigs. In the UK, most gelatin is beef in origin. This makes it unsuitable for vegetarians and vegans.

tip

There are many alternatives to gelatin. The two most commonly used are, gar-agar (it comes from seawood and is used to make vegetarian marshmallows) and pectin (it is usually derived from citrus fruits).

Most medicine and vitamin capsules are also made of gelatin, but liquid forms of the medicines that are free of the substance may be available. For instance, the anti-depressant Prozac comes in gelatin shells, but can also be taken in pure liquid form.

GLYCERIN/GLYCEROL (Glycerine in the UK)

This can come from animal fat, but you can also get vegetarian glycerin. Unless a product specifically states it is vegetable in origin, it's wise to assume it's of the animal variety.

Products that can contain animal glycerin are soap, cosmetics, toothpastes, and some foods, like candies (sweets as they call them in the UK).

Coconut and palm oils are popular sources of vegetable glycerin.

ISINGLASS

You get this from the swim bladder of a fish and it's used as a filtering agent in drinks, both alcoholic and non-alcoholic. The final drink does not contain Isinglass as it's for filtering only, but the fact the fish have to be dead first to get their bladders makes anything filtered with Isinglass not suitable for vegans and vegetarians.

Isinglass is used in the production of Guinness, Lilt (in the UK) and many other alcoholic beverages.

Please note – This is by no means an exhaustive guide and some of the products mentioned as not suitable for vegetarians at the time this was published may have stopped using animal products.

LARD

Lard is animal fat and, as such, isn't suitable for vegetarian or vegans. It used to be popular in the UK as a spread on bread. These days, it can be found mainly in cakes, biscuits and desserts.

tip

Mincemeat and suet may contain lard, but there are vegetarian alternatives to both and as people become more health conscious, lard is no longer as popular as it once was.

VITAMIN D

Cereals are often fortified with this vitamin, which helps to keep bones strong. This vitamin is unusual as you can also get it from sun exposure. But, vegans need to be wary as vitamin D often comes from sheep's wool (this is called D3 or cholecalciferol).

There are vegan suitable supplements of vitamin D available, which come from yeast or mushrooms. When sourced from plant material, it's called D2. Vitamin D is often added to soy (Soya) milk. A deficiency in this vitamin has been linked to cancer and most people don't get enough of the sunshine vitamin.

THINGS THAT DON'T SOUND VEGETARIAN BUT THEY ARE

When you are a vegetarian or a vegan, it can be a nightmare trying to figure out whether something is okay to eat.

CHEESE

Most cheeses these days do not contain animal rennet. Instead, they use a non-animal version that requires no animals to be used.

MEAT FLAVORED POTATO CHIPS (CRISPS)

Of all the questions vegetarians get, this is one of the most common – 'can you eat meat flavored potato chips?'

Many people believe that flavor from real meat is used to flavor potato chips, but that isn't the case. Most flavorings come from artificial sources or from vegetables. For instance, bacon flavored chips may be flavored with beetroot juice. The main type of chips vegetarians need to be on the look out for are cheese flavored ones, because animal rennet might have been used. Fishy flavors should also be avoided, although prawn cocktail flavors are usually artificial.

PREGELATINIZED STARCH

Vegetarians and vegans don't eat gelatin (also spelt gelatine), so seeing this on a label can be a cause for concern. But, this doesn't contain gelatin at all. In fact, it usually comes from maize that has been cooked and dried.

Pregelatinized starch is commonly found in the capsules medicines and vitamins come in, to make them suitable for different diets.

WHEY

This is one of those tricky ingredients you'll find sitting somewhere in the middle of the list, usually in chocolate products. Whey most often comes from the cheese making process where animal rennet is used, so is not suitable for vegetarians never mind vegans. It's also used in some potato chips (crisps in the UK). Unless it specifies that it comes from cow's milk, whey is not suitable for vegetarians or vegans because it involves killing a calf.

WORCESTER SAUCE

This contains anchovies, which are small fish. The good news is that there are vegetarian/vegan versions available. Check the label.

fact

In 2008, the UN recommended that people should have one meat-free day if they wanted to make a difference to climate change. The UN's Food and Agriculture Organization estimated that meat production accounted for nearly a fifth of global greenhouse gas emissions. Much of this was down to cows emitting methane gasses and the resources taken up to producing enough for the cows to eat.

MEAT REDUCERS

Meat reducers are usually people who don't want to give up eating meat completely. They want to cut down, usually for health reasons, because rarely a week goes by without the medical profession and scientists telling us we need to eat less meat and more fruit and vegetables.

Meat reducers tend to fall into three camps –

1. They want to reduce the amount of all meats they consume for health reasons. They may be worried about heart disease, putting on weight, or worry they could 'catch' Bird Flu or Mad cow disease (bovine spongiform encephalopathy), which originated in the UK.

2. They want to stop eating red meat like steak because they think its bad for them. They will probably eat 'white' leaner meats like chicken and turkey instead.

3. They are concerned about animal welfare and factory farming in particular.

WHAT IS MAD COW DISEASE?

Mad cow disease or BSE (bovine spongiform encephalopathy) is a progressive and lethal central nervous system disease in cows that is believed to be man-made. Scientists can tell it is present if they see clear holes in the brains of cows. These holes look like a sponge and that's where spongiform came from.

Scientists believe that BSE was created after cows, who are vegetarian animals, were fed sheep offal (the leftover parts of killed sheep that are considered unfit for human consumption). When the animals died, they, in turn, were put into feed for other animals to eat, which accelerated the spread of the disease.

At its height in the 90's, millions of cows were culled (slaughtered) in the UK and there was a ban on exporting British beef.

The human strain of mad cow disease is called Variant Creutzfeldt-Jakob disease (vCJD) and was first diagnosed in the mid-1990's. Humans contracted it through eating infected beef. It causes neurological problems – usually starting with behavioral changes, insomnia and lack of coordination – and progresses to the patient being unable to talk or move until they eventually lapse into a coma and die.

At the moment, there is no cure and scientists believe that the disease may be lying dormant in many more people and some of them may have been wrongly diagnosed with Alzheimer's, Huntingdon's or dementia, which have similar symptoms.

fact

The disease can lay dormant in cows and humans and can only be conclusively diagnosed by dissecting the brain after death.

WHY EATING LESS MEAT IS GOOD FOR YOU

There are many solid, scientific reasons why cutting down on meat can improve your health and your chances of not getting certain diseases –

1. Most meats tend to be higher in fat than plant protein, which means you are at a higher risk of heart disease if you eat meat, especially fatty meats like steak.

2. Meat can be high in calories. Vegetarians tend to be slimmer than their meat eating counterparts.

3. Meat is harder for the human body to digest than plant protein, which may explain the findings of a European study of 400,000 people that found that the people who ate meat put on more weight than those who didn't, even when they were consuming the same amount of calories.

4. Meat is high in saturated fat, which has been linked with breast and bowel cancer.

5. Those who eat meat regularly are less likely than their vegetarian counterparts to eat enough fruit and vegetables.

6. You're more likely to get food poisoning if you eat meat, especially during barbecue season.

7. You can reduce your cancer risk by cutting down on meat consumption. This may be down to a number of things – the slowness with which meat passes through your body, the drugs the animals you eat were given to fatten them up quicker, and the fact that plants have cancer fighting nutrients and plenty of fiber, amongst others.

fact

In 2009, a US study featured in Archives of Internal Medicine, found that those who consumed large quantities of meat had an increased risk of death from all causes, including cancer and heart disease. The study was conducted over ten years and 500,000 people took part.

In America, The Humane Society of the United States (HSUS) work towards improving the conditions of farm animals. They believe the three components of humane eating are reduce, refine and replace.

1. Reduce – as in reducing the amount of animal products consumed.

2. Refine – as in refining the diet to eat less products from the cruelest production systems, like veal (made by placing calves in crates) and Foie gras (made by force-feeding ducks and geese).

3. Replace – as in replacing animal products, like meat, with plant foods in your diet.

HOW TO REDUCE THE AMOUNT OF MEAT IN YOUR DIET

The easiest way to do this is to have a meat-free day (see below). One day a week when the whole family don't eat meat. A number of family favorites can be adapted to be completely free of meat.

WHAT TO HAVE ON MEAT-FREE DAYS

1. Have a veggie roast – Instead of having a Sunday Roast or the traditional Thanksgiving meat feast, vegetarians can have a nut roast or a chicken, turkey or beef (flavored) Quorn roast, which are just as tasty. The veggie equivalents also contain a lot less calories than the traditional roast. Quorn is widely available in the UK and is flavorsome, very low in fat and fills you up.

2. Spaghetti Bolognese can be made by adding Soy, TVP (textured vegetable protein) or Quorn mince to the spaghetti. The same mince can also be used to make one of Scotland's traditional dishes, stovies. Just add veggie sausages, potatoes and carrot and onion gravy and hey presto, you have a tasty meal without the high fat and calories.

3. How about some pasta? Easy to make and very filling, you can add whatever sauce you like or try making your own using fresh tomatoes and herbs. Very tasty and easy to make.

4. Have a veggie salad. You can have all the vegetables that you want, but instead of the usual ham or tuna, why not try a meat substitute like Quorn or tofu or one of the many mock meats available?

5. Baked potatoes and potato skins are simple to make and you can add any topping you want. Why not have baked beans or cheese and pickle or a nice salad?

6. Many of the vegetarian brands these days have their own fishless products, like fishless fish cakes and mock tuna. Have that instead of your usual fish. Remember that over-fishing is one of the causes of climate change.

7. How about having fun as a family and making your own pizza? You can buy the base from a store or make your own using dough. Add things like peppers, peppercorns, sweetcorn, olives, onions, cheese, tomato, carrot, grilled or fried eggplant (aubergines in the UK), nuts, herbs, artichokes, red peppers, herbs, garlic and zucchini (courgettes). The only limit is your imagination. Your homemade pizza is guaranteed to taste delicious, like everything does when you make it yourself.

8. Have some vegetarian hot dogs. It's not just vegetarians who say they taste better than the meat version, which is usually made from mechanically separated meat: the poorest quality of meat.

9. Curries are fantastic, too. There are so many variations and traditionally, in India where curries originate from, meat is rarely used because many people are Hindus (most of whom are vegetarian) or the meat is of such poor quality that no one eats it.

10. And, if its fast food you want, why not ditch the Big Mac for a tasty veggie burger. You can get all kinds: spicy, nutty, hot, sweet or regular.

CONSIDERING GOING VEGETARIAN OR VEGAN?

See 'Vegetarian & Vegan Organizations' for a list of some helpful sites at the back of the book under 'Useful Websites.' There are so many free and helpful resources available.

Cruelty Free Cosmetics

" I am not interested to know whether vivisection produces results that are profitable to the human race or doesn't...The pain which it inflicts upon un-consenting animals is the basis of my enmity toward it, and it is to me sufficient justification of the enmity without looking further. "

Mark Twain

Chapter 5
Cruelty Free Cosmetics

The testing of cosmetics on animals has always been a very conscientious issue. On one hand, there are those who say that unless this testing is carried out, cosmetics will not be safe for human use, and humans should come first before animals.

On the other hand, there are those who insist that there is no need to test products like foundation and perfumes on animals because it's cruel and unethical. They also argue that cosmetics are for vanity reasons and are not essential.

It is the second opinion that seems to be the most popular even amongst people who are not vegetarian or vegan. So popular, in fact, that in 2013, in the European Union, most cosmetics testing will be banned.

America will not be following suit, although there have been calls for them to adopt the same ban, by animal welfare charities such as The American Anti-vivisection Society and PETA.

fact
In a 2010 YouGov poll conducted in the UK, 60% of those asked said they didn't think cosmetics should be tested on animals.

ANIMAL TESTING & THE LAW

America

Cosmetics testing used to be unregulated in America until 1938, when congress gave the *FDA* (*The Food and Drug Administration*) the right to regulate cosmetics. For the purposes of the 1938 Act, cosmetics were defined as products for 'cleansing, beautifying, promoting attractiveness, or altering the appearance.'

This was in no small part due to an incident that took place in 1933 in the country. Women used mascara called *Lush Lure*, which was supposed to make their lashes look darker. The product worked, but had catastrophic side effects. Some women suffered from eye irritation, whilst others were blinded and one person died.

The side effects were attributed to *paraphenylenediamine*, a chemical extremely toxic to the body, which was used as the dye agent in the mascara. However, after this substance was found to be toxic, it would no longer be used.

fact

There is currently no legal requirement for cosmetics to be tested on animals in America. They do, however, have a duty for companies to prove that their products aren't toxic or pose a threat to public safety. This can be done without animal testing.

Canada

There is no legal obligation to test cosmetics on animals. For the purposes of the law, cosmetics are defined as 'a product which cleanses, improves or alters the complexion, skin, hair or teeth.'

Australia

It's illegal to test cosmetics on animals in Australia, but this doesn't mean all cosmetics on sale are cruelty free. To get round the no testing law, companies have their products tested abroad in countries like China. This is a common situation worldwide where a country will ban animal testing on cosmetics in their own country, but not ban the importing of animal tested products.

For more information on the ban on testing cosmetics on animals in Australia, visit **www.animalsaustralia.org/take_action/ban-animal-tested-products**

The UK

The testing of products and ingredients on animals was banned in the UK in 1998.

There are still cosmetics on sale in the UK that have been tested on animals. These tests have been done outside the UK. This is the loophole many companies use to beat the ban.

`fact`

The bulk of animal cosmetics testing, these days, is carried out in China, where labor is cheap and there are few laws governing animal welfare. In China, all cosmetics that are sold in China must undergo animal testing. This includes products made outside China that are imported to China.

The European Union ban

On 11 March 2009, the European Union (EU), of which the UK is a member, enacted an amendment to its Cosmetics Directive that implemented a partial ban on the sale anywhere in the EU of cosmetics and toiletries containing ingredients which have been tested on animals. This meant that cosmetic companies wouldn't be able to sell cosmetics tested on animals even when the testing was done outside the EU.

In 2013 there is to be an EU wide ban on cosmetics testing on animals, but this only bans certain tests where alternatives are available and not all animal testing.

For instance, animal testing could still be allowed on ingredients used in cosmetics that are considered to be needed to meet requirements of other laws, like anti-pollution laws.

" The EU has banned all animal tests for cosmetic ingredients, formulations, and final products. In addition, the sale of cosmetics and ingredients that have been tested on animals, regardless of where the testing occurred, is also prohibited, with the exception of three test areas (repeated-dose toxicity, reproductive toxicity, and toxicokinetics). The final three test areas will be banned in March 2013. "

Source – The EU website*

---

* There is a threat to this ban and animal rights groups are working to ensure it comes into being.

WHAT TESTS ARE DONE ON ANIMALS?

The most common tests carried out on animals are:

1. Draize Skin Tests

In this test, animals such as rabbits, mice and rats have their fur shaved and then they have the cosmetic product, like shampoo or make up, rubbed into the area.

Why they do this: to see if there is any damage or irritation to the area. This is meant to predict how the product will react on human skin.

Why anti-vivisectionists oppose this:

- It's cruel and causes unnecessary pain and suffering to the animals used.

- It will not predict how the product will react on humans.

- On most products it will say 'not to use on irritated or broken skin.'

2. Draize Eye Tests

Of all animal tests for cosmetics, these are considered the cruelest.

White albino rabbits are used because they are unable to wash away irritable substances from their eyes. Their heads are immobilized, so they cannot move, and then different chemicals are dripped into their eyes and left there to see how their eyes react. Researchers then check their eyes for any irritation or damage.

This test is used for both cosmetics and household products, like washing powder and bleach, and was devised because of the *Lush Lure* incident.

Why they do this: like the skin test, any damage or irritation to the area is recorded. This is meant to predict how the product will react in human eyes.

Why anti-vivisectionists oppose this:

- There is a huge difference between rabbits' eyes and humans. For instance, we produce a lot more tears than the rabbits used in these tests, which are chosen specifically because they produce so few tears.

- The tests are painful for the rabbits who are given no form of pain relief.

- Animals, unlike humans, cannot tell you how they are feeling.

- The contraptions used to confine the rabbits and to keep them still are like some form of medieval torture device.

3. Lethal Dose Tests (LD50 Tests)

Animals are force-fed substances (usually by having a tube forced down their throats) or they are injected with them, or made to inhale them to see just how much will kill them. LF50 stands for the lethal dose it will take to kill 50 percent of the test subjects. Animals usually vomit, suffer convulsions, are paralyzed and have bleeding from the skin, nose, eyes and mouth.

Why they do this: To evaluate how toxic something is and to hopefully relate that data to humans.

Why anti-vivisectionists oppose this:

- It's a horrific and painful way for animals to die.

- It does not guarantee what the lethal dose is in humans, who will react in a different way as we are genetically different. Not to mention much larger.

- The tests don't result in safer products. Often personal care products that carry warnings about causing skin irritation and allergic reactions are still made available for sale, which makes you wonder why they bother to put animals through grueling tests to find that out.

IS IT POSSIBLE TO TEST PRODUCTS SAFELY WITHOUT USING ANIMALS?

In a word, yes. A number of tests have been developed. The development of these tests is very important as they can also be used to test drugs and other chemicals. This speeds up research.

Here are the most commonly used ones:

1. PETA (People for the Ethical Treatment of Animals) helped fund the development of the cruelty-free skin irritation test. No animals are used in this test. Instead, they are replaced with three-dimensional reconstructions of human skin using cells grown in culture. This test is now widely used and considered to be more accurate and efficient than testing on animals.

2. Human Patch Tests – These are conducted on human volunteers and, because of that, they are more reliable than animal testing.

In Canada, these tests are conducted on human volunteers who are considered a valid replacement for skin irritation studies on animals. However, skin patch tests are only used after scientists first confirm that chemicals are not corrosive, using another non-animal method and various computer modeling and test tube studies to make sure that any patch test done uses chemicals that are not obvious irritants.

3. Eyetex™

Unlike the Draize eye tests, rabbits aren't used; a vegetable dye that reacts to any irritants like the cornea of the human eye is used in their place. This test is considered to be more reliable than the Draize eye test. This is because, in the Draize test, people have to estimate the damage caused, meaning results are all down to human error and are not exact. With Eyetex™, more accurate information is obtained because the results can be measured by a machine called a spectrophotometer.

HOW DO YOU TELL IF A PRODUCT IS CRUELTY FREE?

It has never been easier to buy products that are cruelty free. This is because of the introduction of clear labeling. There are clear logos placed on products that make it clear that these products are not tested on animals and neither are their ingredients.

THE LEAPING BUNNY LOGO

Cruelty free products carry what is known as the 'Leaping Bunny' logo, which is also known as The Humane Cosmetics Standard (HCS) and Humane Household Products Standard (HHPS). This is administered by The Coalition for Consumer Information on Cosmetics (CCIC) who do onsite checks of any company wishing to use their logo. This logo is recognized In America, Canada, most European countries and the UK.

To earn the right to display this cruelty free standard on their products, the makers of cosmetics, toiletries, baby products and household products, must show that the particular product was made without any animal testing and that includes the ingredients, the final product and any stage of its development.

Only companies that are approved are allowed to carry the famous leaping bunny logo and they get to be listed on both the online and published Compassionate Shopping Guide.

Visit their website at – **www.leapingbunny.org** for more details. **www.gocrueltyfree.org** also carries the same information.

THE BRITISH APPROVED BUNNY LOGO

In the UK, products carry the same Leaping Bunny logo with the addition of 'BUAV approved,' which means that neither the ingredients nor the final product were tested on animals. The BUAV is the British Union for the Abolition of Vivisection. As well as campaigning against all animal testing, they also do undercover investigations and political lobbying.

BUAV
APPROVED

Visit their website at – **www.buav.org** for further details.

Any company that has their logo on their products must meet the same strict guidelines as the Leaping Bunny mark. In the UK, all of Superdrug's own brand products carry this logo.

The BUAV also produce the free pocket guide 'The Little Book of Cruelty Free' listing cruelty free companies who qualify to put their logo on products.

You can also visit the BUAV spin off website for details at – **www. gocrueltyfree.org**

tip

PETA (The People's Ethical Treatment for Animals) provides a list of cruelty free companies on their website at peta.org (they cover US & UK companies, as well as world brands). However, their criteria for being on the list aren't as stringent as the Leaping Bunny ones.

tip

The Vegan's Society produces the Animal Free Shopper Guide for vegans in the UK. Check it out at – **www.vegansociety.com**

WHAT ARE FIXED CUT OFF DATES?

Companies, who carry the Leaping Bunny mark, operate a 'fixed cut-off date' (FCOD) policy for animal testing. This means that, after a certain date, they don't conduct any animal tests, and have a policy of not using any ingredients tested on animals by their suppliers from a fixed date.

The FCOD is the most widely accepted non-animal testing policy and the most reliable.

'THIS PRODUCT IS NOT TESTED ON ANIMALS' OR 'IS CRUELTY FREE'

Some products may not carry these logos and still say they are 'not tested on animals.' However, this may mean that the final product has not been tested on animals, but the ingredients are. Or, that the suppliers of their ingredients do test them on animals.

If you are unsure, always ask before you buy. You have every right to be fully informed.

tip

Not all of the companies, who would qualify for the Leaping Bunny logo or to get some form of cruelty free accreditation, apply. You may have to do your own research before you buy.

WHY IS THE LEAPING BUNNY TRADEMARK THE BEST?

The Leaping Bunny logo, which is used throughout the world, currently is the only one that guarantees a final product and the ingredients it contains have not been tested on animals by that company and that the ingredients have not been tested on animals by their suppliers. Other companies may have a similar logo on their products, including that of a rabbit (as there is no copyright on that), but that can be very misleading and does not guarantee they are cruelty free.

Example – Say a company called All Creatures don't test their products or ingredients on animals, but they do buy, use and benefit financially from chemical ingredients that have recently been tested on animals by their suppliers. They would quite rightly not be on the list of companies that qualify for the Humane Cosmetic Standard and Humane Household Standard, which allows them to use the Leaping Bunny trademark (these qualifying companies must allow various checks to be made).

Companies who do qualify don't conduct animal testing or use ingredients from companies that do animal testing and must show that this has been the case for five years (that's what's known as a 'fixed cut off date'). Therefore, our made up company wouldn't qualify.

Note – other cruelty free lists may be less strict than the Leaping Bunny one.

OTHER RABBIT & NO ANIMAL TESTING LOGOS

Products may often carry a rabbit or similar cruelty free logo, making you think they are cruelty free, but this may not be the case. Or they may say one of the following:

1. **'This product contains no animal ingredients.'** Reading this, you may be misled into thinking this product is cruelty free, but this simply means what it says and does not tell you anything about whether it's tested on animals.

2. **'Neither this product or its ingredients are tested on animals.'** This appears on products that often feature a rabbit type logo that's not the same as the Leaping Bunny version. It may be these items genuinely are cruelty free and that the company either doesn't want to carry the guaranteed cruelty free logo, or hasn't yet qualified for it as they need to prove that they haven't tested the finished products or the ingredients on animals for five years and that their suppliers haven't either. Or, perhaps they are simply unaware that they can apply.

3. **'This product is not tested on animals.'** Note – it says nothing about the ingredients not being tested on animals.

HOW DO I CHECK IF A COMPANY OR ITS PRODUCTS ARE CRUELTY FREE?

Do they have the Leaping Bunny logo on their products? If you don't find one then the chances are they are not cruelty free. Either, consult the lists on the Leaping Bunny (**www.leapingbunny.org**) or go cruelty free sites (**www.gocrueltyfree.org**) – they have lists of companies worldwide who don't test on animals, or contact the company direct and ask just what their policy is on animal testing. The more people who do that, the more likely companies will get the message that consumers want cruelty free cosmetics.

The Australian site **www.choosecrueltyfree.org.au** is the number one site for Australians who want to go cruelty free.

tip

Big companies may claim to be 'against animal testing,' on their websites and leaflets, but unless they are on a reliable cruelty free list or carry a Leaping Bunny logo on their products, there's a good chance they use animal testing.

" *Whenever people say, 'We mustn't be sentimental,' you can take it they are about to do something cruel. And if they add, 'We must be realistic,' they mean they are going to make money out of it.* **"**

Brigid Brophy, English-Irish novelist and playwright

MYTHS ABOUT CRUELTY FREE COSMETICS

To justify testing cosmetics on animals, companies may come up with seemingly good reasons why they do test. But these are generally myths.

1. Without animal testing, products can't be safe

Not testing on animals doesn't mean no testing at all. In fact, it may mean more reliable testing, because, instead of animals, human skin grown in test tubes may be used. Skin patch tests on humans who can tell the testers how they are feeling can also be used.

Researchers can also tell whether products will be safe by using ingredients already known to be safe.

2. No animal testing means less effective products

Not so. Many big name cruelty free companies, like Mary Kay and Urban Decay, produce some of the most popular cosmetics sold. Ones that win awards and celebrities are proud to boast of using. They don't test on animals.

3. The law requires animal testing

No, it doesn't. In the US, neither the U.S. Food and Drug Administration (FDA) nor the U.S. Consumer Product Safety Commission require animal testing for cosmetics or household products. There is enough existing information to make testing for products obsolete.

When companies tell you they must carry out animal testing by law, it's a lie. They may be using new ingredients, which under the law need to have been tested before they go on sale, but this does not have to be on animals.

Cell cultures could be used, or human skin generated in a test tube, or even human volunteers. There are so many alternatives to using animals.

ALL PRODUCTS CARRYING THE BUNNY LOGO ARE SUITABLE FOR VEGETARIANS AND VEGANS

This is a common misconception. The Leaping Bunny certification is a guarantee of no animal testing, not of no animal products having been used, like gelatine (it comes from the inside of animals' skin and bones), animal glycerin (made from animal fats), collagen (usually from fish, although you can get synthetic collagen), tallow (from bones), and cochineal (crushed insects who produce a reddish/pinkish color found in cosmetics).

To ensure products are suitable for vegetarians or vegans and that they don't contain any animal products, like fish oil, check the labeling for the 'V' for vegetarian symbol or vegan logo. There are different variations of the suitable for vegans' logo, but they generally have the word 'vegan' included.

tip

In the case of vegetarian, they may have just a simple 'V' or a 'V' sign with the wording 'Vegetarian Society approved' written above it. The Vegetarian Society is the most reliable of all vegetarian logos as products that carry the logo (food, household products, confectionery and cosmetics) are scrupulously checked.

tip

If suitable for vegans, they may carry an approved by the Vegan Society logo. You can search for vegetarian and vegan products at the **www. gocrueltyfree.org** site by selecting the Vegan/Vegetarian Society Approved options as you search.

Note – The reverse is also true. Just because a product has the appropriate vegan or vegetarian symbol does not mean it's not tested on animals.

ETHICAL CLEANING AND HOUSEHOLD PRODUCTS

It's not only food and cosmetics that can involve cruel animal testing. Many things we use everyday, like washing powder, air fresheners, window cleaners, toilet cleaners and furniture polish are usually tested on animals: both the ingredients and the finished product.

If you want to avoid buying household products, including cleaners and toiletries, that are tested on animals, then there is a site that lists cruelty free companies at **www.gocrueltyfree.org**

You can search by country, including the USA, Canada, Australia, the UK, Singapore, Ireland, India and South Africa. In some countries, brands are only available online.

You can also search by either cosmetics or household products.

fact

In the UK in 2008, the BUAV (the British Union for the Abolition of Vivisection) launched a campaign to end the use of animals in the testing of household products. Their campaign is fittingly called Clean Up Cruelty. The campaign has gained support from politicians, retailers and the public.

fact

In the UK, certified cruelty free household products and cleaners (they carry the BUAV Leaping Bunny logo) are made by stores like the Co-op and Marks and Spencer. Other top brands include Astonish, Method and Faith In Nature.

Shop Kind

" Slavery can only be abolished by raising the character of the people who compose the nation; and that can be done only by showing them a higher one. "

Maria W Chapman, slavery abolitionists

Chapter 6
Shop Kind

These days, more and more people want to be ethical shoppers because they want to know that the things they buy were produced by workers who were paid a fair price for their wares.

This chapter is devoted to ethical shopping and the various schemes to ensure producers of goods get treated fairly, because being cruelty free means not being cruel to our fellow human beings, too.

WHAT IS AN ETHICAL SHOPPER?

Normally, ethical shoppers want to know if:

- Products are tested on animals.

- Products were produced using slave labor or child labor.

- Products were made by workers who were paid a fair wage.

- Products were made by workers who had decent working conditions, i.e. they weren't over-worked or made to work in a factory without proper ventilation.

- Products were made from sustainable materials that are not going to run out and cause environmental problems, such as pollution and damage to the Ozone layer.

- Where relevant, if products are made from recycled materials and the packaging can be recycled. That way the packaging doesn't end up in a landfill site.

HOW TO BECOME AN ETHICAL SHOPPER

Being an ethical shopper isn't always easy. Often it isn't until you read about a company using slave labor and child labor that you become aware of the fact that they have questionable ethics.

There is one way to guarantee that goods are ethical and that is by buying Fair Trade certified products (just called Fairtrade in the UK).

The UK's leading alternative consumer organization have a website at **www.ethicalconsumer.org** where brands are awarded points according to 5 different criteria:

1. environment (does the production of this product result in damage to the environment)

2. animals (was the product tested on animals, a product of factory farming and was animal welfare taken into account)

3. people (human and workers rights, irresponsible marketing and does the company profit from the arms trade)

4. politics (have there been calls to boycott the country's products, does the company use genetic engineering, etc.)

5. product sustainability (is the product Fairtrade, organic, was animal welfare and the environment taken into account)

Note – Although this is a UK-based site, the information applies to many global brands that you can buy elsewhere in the world, like America, Canada and South Africa.

MODERN-DAY SLAVERY

Slavery is meant to have been abolished, yet millions of workers throughout the world wouldn't know it. Under-paid and over-worked, forced to work and live in conditions people in the West would consider shocking, slave laborers are living the modern-day equivalent of slavery.

Slave labor can happen anywhere. In 2011, it emerged that a 38-year-old Filipino woman was kept as a domestic slave by a Vancouver couple who brought her over from Hong Kong. They forced her to work all the time and emotionally and physically abused her. There have been several similar cases in the UK and the USA. Unscrupulous employees often stop people from leaving by hiding their passports or threatening to report them to the authorities.

In Dubai, in the United Arab Emirates, most of the luxury accommodation built was the work of hundreds of thousands of Asian workers who were paid low salaries and forced to exist in squalor. Many of them came from places like India where they fled poverty. Many were recruited by unscrupulous recruitment firms who charged them hefty fees to come to the country. Source – Human Rights Watch.

Here are some more sobering statistics:

- According to Anti-slavery International, millions of men, women and children throughout the world are forced to live as slaves. We may not think of these people as slaves, but that's exactly what they are. Exploited by being forced to work for little pay, they are often sold as though they are objects and not people. This is often done by traffickers who force people to work as some form of repayment for getting them into another country. This is called forced labor and is a form of slave labor.

- According to International Labour Organization (ILO) estimates, there are at least 12.3 million people in forced labor worldwide. A staggering 40-50 percent of them are children.

- Figures from the US State Department claimed that an estimated 17,500 people are trafficked into the country every year, but this is only an estimate, as the true figure is not known. Many of them are used as forced labor.

- In 2009, budget high street chain Primark in the UK was accused of using slave labor. In a joint operation with the BBC, illegal immigrants were found to be working in sweatshops in Manchester for half the minimum wage payable by law.

WHAT IS A SWEAT SHOP?

The term was first heard in 1892 in reference to clothes makers in the USA and the atrocious working conditions they endured.

It's estimated that millions of people throughout the world work in poor, often unsanitary conditions, for long hours and very low pay. The problem is made worse by the practice of large companies contracting out work to countries that have poor labor laws. That way their labor costs will be low and their profit margins high.

These days, although the conditions may have improved, sweatshops are guilty of labor violations. Things like using child labor and forcing workers to work on long after they should be allowed to go home, and often for no extra pay, just to meet targets. Note – in many cases, sweatshop employers provide accommodation for their employees that is well below what we could consider a habitable standard (many people forced to share a single room, no toilet facilities or access to water for washing, etc.) and they deduct the rent from their pitiful wages.

Sadly, sweatshops are not just a problem in developing nations like India, there have also been instances of sweatshops in the USA, UK and Canada, in what could rightly be termed modern day slavery.

Sweatshops in the West tend to employ vulnerable people who have no choice but to work for them. People like single mothers, asylum seekers and those in the country illegally.

WHAT IS FAIR TRADE?

Fair Trade is the perfect name for it because the scheme means exactly what it says, namely that a fair trade is made.

This means:

1. The farmers are paid a fair price

2. The workers are paid a fair price

Fairtrade first appeared in the 1980's when coffee produced in Mexico was given the Fairtrade label and sold in Dutch supermarkets.

By the late 80's and early 90's, the brand was sold in stores in the USA and Canada (under the Transfair label) and the UK (with the Fairtrade mark on the packaging), Japan and France amongst others.

tip

The Fair Trade certification and Fairtrade labels now appear on a diverse variety of products, like bananas, fruit juices, clothing, footballs, roses and chocolate.

WHAT IS THE FAIR TRADE LOGO?

To make sure its Fair Trade, always look out for the distinctive label that says it's Fair Trade. In America, the label is a white square that says 'Fair Trade USA' and then 'every purchase matters.'

In the UK, the Fairtrade label is a distinctive blue, green, white and black logo. When some people see it, they say it looks like a parrot or a leaf. The most popular interpretation is that the green represents grass, the blue the sky and the black dot and swirl a person with their hand raised aloft. It reads 'Fairtrade Foundation' below the logo.

In Canada, the logo is the same as the UK logo except it reads 'Fairtrade' at the bottom. There is also another logo that is a rectangle with 'Fair Trade certified' at the top and 'certified equitable' along the bottom. The logo for this one is a person (half white and half black) holding a bowl in either hand.

To learn more about Fair Trade certified products in the USA,
visit **www.transfairusa.org**
To learn more Fair Trade in Canada, go to **http://fairtrade.ca**
For the UK, go to **www.fairtrade.org.uk**
For South Africa, visit **www.fairtrade.org.za**
For Australia and New Zealand, visit **www.fta.org.au**

tip

If you want to buy genuine Fairtrade, it doesn't have to carry the label. You can buy it when you're on holiday simply by buying souvenirs from local people in street markets instead of in shopping complexes or in hotel shops.

fact

A product carrying the Fair Trade (Fairtrade logo) doesn't mean that the company who produced it didn't use slave labor or child labor to make their other products. It refers to that product only.

fact

In 2003, Fair Trade oranges from South Africa were put on the market.

fact

The fastest growth in Fair Trade products has been in coffee beans and in cocoa beans. This is because of the boom in coffee and chocolate sales.

HOW DO FAIR TRADE/FAIRTRADE ENSURE WORKERS ARE TREATED FAIRLY?

Producers are inspected by an organization called FLO-CERT who check to make sure that producers are contributing to the social and economic development through people's purchases. They are an independent company who offer Fairtrade certification to clients in more than 70 countries. To learn more about them visit **www.flo-cert.net** and click on 'English.'

WHERE CAN I BUY FAIR TRADE/FAIRTRADE?

Most supermarket chains will sell at least some products carrying the certification, even if it's only chocolate, coffee or bananas.

Big name brands that sell Fair Trade products include Starbucks, Ben & Jerry's and Divine Chocolate.

The UK is one of the largest markets for Fairtrade products. Most stores, like Marks and Spencer, Asda and the Co-Op, will sell Fairtrade coffee, chocolate and bananas.

There are also lists of stockists on the Fairtrade websites.

IS FAIRTRADE EXPENSIVE?

Yes, it can be when compared to other products, but ask yourself this: is knowing that the workers who toiled to produce what you bought were paid fairly not worth the extra cost?

WHY IS THE FAIR TRADE LABEL NEEDED?

- All over the world, farmers and workers are being exploited in some of the poorest countries.

- Fair Trade raises the standard of living for workers throughout the world.

- Fair Trade raises the salaries of workers so they can afford to feed their families.

- Fair Trade prevents people in countries from being paid too little for the things they produce. In many countries, people starve not because they don't produce anything to sell, but because they aren't paid a fair price for what they do produce.

- Fair Trade helps improve people's working conditions.

- Because consumers genuinely want to know that workers weren't exploited.

CHILD LABOR

Another reason why Fair Trade is needed is to prevent the use of child labor.

According to the organization, Stop Child Labor, there are 218million child laborers in the world. That's 218million children who won't get to go to school. 218million children, who are being exploited and who don't get to live a normal life. And that's just an estimate. The number may be much higher.

HOW CAN YOU KNOW SOMETHING WAS PRODUCED BY CHILD LABOR?

Unfortunately, you can't tell whether child labor was used just by looking at the product. If it carries the Fair Trade label, child labor will probably not have been used as the reason children are used is to provide cheap labor. Gaining the Fair Trade certification guarantees that farmers and workers are treated fairly.

If you're worried that child labor may have been used, ask the store. They may not know or might not tell you the truth, but you have the right to ask. Every consumer has a right to know what they are buying.

HOW CAN I MAKE SURE THE COMPANY I BUY FROM DOESN'T EXPLOIT SLAVE LABOR OR CHILDREN WHEN THEY DON'T HAVE THE FAIR TRADE CERTIFICATION?

1. *Ask the company if they belong to the ETI (Ethical Trading Initiative). Member companies unite with volunteer organizations and trade unions and work towards improving the lives of workers. Read more about it here **www.ethicaltrade.org**

2. *Ask what steps they have taken to ensure that their goods are not made by people who are underpaid and forced to work in poor conditions or by child labor. For instance, do they monitor the factories and the conditions that people work in? This is important because too often companies may contract out to self-employed agents or contractors and not directly find manufacturers themselves. Yet every company has a responsibility to know the ins and outs of its supply chain. As a consumer, you are perfectly entitled to know where the goods you buy or are about to buy come from.

3. *Ask what steps they have taken to ensure that the raw materials used in their products were ethically sourced. Was the cocoa used in their chocolate products or the cotton in their t-shirts farmed by workers paid a fair wage? Unfortunately, many companies don't always have this information, although their suppliers will.

4. Ask if they paid a fair price for the goods. When companies don't and drive the prices down, it's usually the workers who suffer by being asked to work longer for less in worse conditions.

5. Carpets and rugs carrying the 'GoodWeave' certification label and logo weren't made using illegal child labor. The mark used to be 'Rugmark' but this changed in 2009. Read more about it in the international scheme here **www.goodweave.org.uk/about-goodweave/about-goodweave.shtml**. They also have a list of retailers on their website.

*Note – You will probably need to write to head office to get this information, as staff might not be informed. If you don't get a reply that tells you what you want to know, then you can assume this company either isn't an ethical one or doesn't care enough to reply to potential customers.

TRAFFICKED PEOPLE

Slave labor doesn't always mean groups of people being forced to work for low wages in their own countries. It can also mean vulnerable people being brought or coming voluntarily to countries where we think there's no slavery. Many of these people are women and girls forced into the sex trade once they arrive (many are smuggled into the country) and they are what we would call trafficked. This is a very complex topic that would take a book of its own to cover.

If you live in the USA, report suspected trafficking to the Department of Health and Human Services (they have a 24hr hotline) and the Department of Justice sponsored Trafficking in Persons and Worker Exploitation Task Force Complaint Line (a toll free 24hr hotline).

For more details on human trafficking in the USA and non-governmental organizations, advice and contact details, you can go to **www.humantrafficking.org**

In some cases, the victims of trafficking may be given permanent immigration status.

In the UK, Canada and Australia, contact the police.

DOMESTIC SLAVES

Other people may be enticed to come and live in countries like the USA, Canada and the UK with the promise of a good job and salary. Once they arrive, they discover that rather than earn good money as an au pair, nanny or housekeeper, they have to live in people's homes and are treated like domestic slaves. They may also be subjected to physical and mental abuse on a regular basis.

Generally, these people have come of their own free will and are not trafficked, but once they arrive and find out they've been lied to about the kind of life they will lead, it's too late to leave. They may be prevented from leaving by their employer taking their passport or not paying them the salary they've worked for.

Employers may also use the threat of contacting immigration and having them deported; something that would terrify anyone who's living in a strange country, even if they do have a visa. They may also lie about their employee stealing from them to frighten them into staying.

HOW TO SPOT A DOMESTIC SLAVE

- Are they allowed to leave their work site alone to do things like go and buy groceries, or are they always accompanied by someone from the household?

- Do they ever get a day off? Most employees should get at least one day off a week. Have you ever seen them out and about on their own? Say at a movie or out shopping.

- Do they look like they are living in fear? Are they nervous or jumpy?

- Have they been threatened by anyone in the household?

- Have you seen any evidence that they've been assaulted? Bruises, cuts, broken bones, torn clothes?

- Are they shabbily dressed/always wearing the same clothes? This is a sign they are not being paid a decent salary or even any salary at all. Often employers make 'deductions' from their salaries for breakages, food and board when they've got no right to do that.

- Do they have a contract of employment that details their terms and conditions? Are they paid the minimum wage or much less?

- Are they ever allowed to use the phone and, when they do, is someone always listening in?

- Do they ever get any mail? If they don't, this might be a sign that they are not allowed to contact anyone.

fact

The majority of cases of domestic slavery in the USA are never prosecuted. The victims are too scared; they can't speak the language and are ashamed of what's happened to them.

fact

In 2010, over 15,000 domestic workers were brought to the UK. Charities claim that many end up as slaves working for rich families. Many are paid a pittance, whilst others may have their salaries withheld for no good reason. Their passports may also be confiscated by their employers to prevent them from leaving.

WHAT YOU CAN DO TO HELP

If you suspect that someone is being kept as a domestic slave, there are things you can do:

- If you believe someone is a domestic slave, try and talk to them and tell them that they have rights. For instance, their employer has no right to take away their passport. They also have a right to get paid a decent wage.

- Ask them to write down everything that happens to them in their employer's house, such as details of how long they work and any abuse they are subjected to, both mental and physical.

- If you hear them being physical harmed or see any evidence that they have been assaulted, call the police immediately.

- Get numbers for women's shelters (refuges) as most domestic slaves are female. The most important thing is to get them out of the situation. If you live in the UK, contact your local citizen's advice bureau for details.

- If their employer is withholding the person's passport or visa to prevent them from leaving, get the police involved. Often a visit from the police will make employers hand over passports they have no right to have in the first place.

tip

If you live in the USA, contact The American Civil Liberties Union (ACLU) for advice. They have affiliates in every US state and Puerto Rico and can offer legal advice. Go to **www.aclu.org/affiliates** for details.

tip

If you live in the UK, there is a charity called Kalayaan who help migrant domestic workers. See **www.kalayaan.org.uk** for details.

tip

Many of the domestic workers in Canada are Filipino and come to the country through the Live in Caregiver program. PINAY is a Filipino Women's Organization that offers them advice. Contact **pinaycan@yahoo.com**

19 Ways to Create a More Compassionate World

"" Progress is impossible without change, and those who cannot change their minds cannot change anything. ""

George Bernard Shaw

Chapter 7

19 Ways to Create a More Compassionate World

Famine. War. Child abuse. Animal cruelty. It can be distressing seeing all the bad things that go on in the world and feeling a sense of hopelessness.

Where do you begin to make a difference? To change things and make it a better world for everyone?

The good news is that we can all live a more compassionate life with the choices we make. Whether it's donating money to charities that give people the means to feed themselves, deciding not to go on holiday to a region of Spain where they still have bullfighting, or looking out for our elderly neighbors, we can all do something to create a better world for us all to live in. And we can start today.

Here are some easy ways to live cruelty free.

1. SUPPORT WORLD VISION'S MICRO SCHEME

The charity World Vision run a micro-finance program where they offer loans to people in developing countries such as Rwanda, the Philippines, Cambodia and Armenia to set up in business. The money goes towards things like stock and land for people who want to set up a business, or need money to continue with an existing business. You decide which entrepreneur you wish to support (there are profiles of would be business people on the site, along with a graph of how much money they need) and you donate however much you can afford, with a minimum of $25.

You also get to track your chosen person's progress and so feel part of what they are doing.

To find out more, visit **www.worldvisionmicro.org**

Canada

They also have a similar scheme in Canada. The minimum donation is $5 Canadian Dollars. Visit World Vision Canada at **www.worldvision.ca/give-a-gift/Pages/howmicroloanswork.aspx**

UK

In the UK, this is called the 'microloans' scheme and is limited to entrepreneurs in five countries. You browse the people looking for loans and decide what you can pay and do it over 12 monthly installments. For instance, one person who ran a food store was looking for a total loan of £180 and the installments were £15 a month.

Read about it here **http://microloans.worldvision.org.uk**

Australia

In Australia, World Vision have something called social and economic empowerment (SEE Solutions projects) where you can give money to individuals and communities to make them self-sufficient and to find out more, visit **www.worldvision.com.au** and put 'loans' in the search box.

fact

Most of the businesses that get micro-finance repay their loans and the money goes back into the scheme, so the money you pay in will keep on working, ensuring that people in poor countries can keep building a better life for themselves and their children.

2. AVOID BUYING COSMETICS THAT CONTAIN CRUELLY OBTAINED INGREDIENTS

In 2011, Lush Cosmetics launched a week long campaign at its stores in Hong Kong and Macau (like Hong Kong, its one of the regions governed by China) to highlight the plight of sharks. The reason a cosmetics company decided to take this action was because, as well as being killed for their flesh (to go in shark fin soup) and cartilage (as an ingredient for health supplements like Chondroitin), sharks are also being killed for their oil, which is used in creams and lotions and Omega 3 fish oil supplements. This shark liver oil contains squalene and pristane, as well as Omega 3 fatty acids.

tip
Shark liver oil can also be called Squalamine.

fact
Sharks are usually killed by being harpooned and dragged through the water, whilst in agony. They suffocate when dragged out of the water.

fact
Many of the sharks that are hunted for their oil are endangered species.

3. AVOID BUYING CHEAP CLOTHING BECAUSE IT MAY COME AT A HUMAN COST

The explosion in cheap clothing may be good for consumers, but it's certainly not good for workers who make the garments and don't get a fair salary for doing it.

Everybody loves a bargain, but sometimes the reason stores can afford to sell things like clothing so cheaply is because the people who make those items are paid so little. This may not always be with the stores' knowledge as many of them rely on agencies to recruit workers, mainly in countries like India and Malaysia, but they still have a duty to make sure their products are ethically sourced.

fact

Fair Trade clothing recently arrived in the USA. To find out more about Transfer USA Fair Trade Certified label go to **www.ecouterre.com/first-fair-trade-certified-clothing-arrives-in-the-us**

tip

As much as possible, try and buy clothing that carries the Fair Trade certification logo, or says Fairtrade on it. That way you can ensure workers are not being taken advantage of.

If you are unable to do that, as in some countries Fair Trade clothing is difficult if not impossible to find, buy clothes that carry an 'ethical' label or say they were made with Fairtrade/Fair Trade certified cotton.

Another good way to make sure whoever produced what you buy has made a fair wage from their work is to buy jewelry and clothes from trade fairs, where people have made it themselves.

tip

There are online stores where you can buy Fair Trade clothing, such as **www.fairindigo.com** and **www.anniegreenabelle.com**, a store that will ship throughout the USA and the UK.

You may also find **www.sweatfree.org/shoppingguide** useful as it offers a range of sweatshop free apparel.

Canada

In Canada, it is possible to buy garments made of Fair Trade cotton. Look out for those labels. Find out more by going to **http://fairtrade.ca/en/products/cotton**

" How wonderful it is that nobody need wait a single moment before starting to improve the world. "

Anne Frank

UK

If you live in the UK, you'll find a list of places where you can buy Fairtrade cotton garments: **www.fairtrade.org.uk/products/cotton/stockists.aspx**. Popular stores like Topman, Sainsbury's, Marks and Spencer and Tesco.

Australia

For more information on Fairtrade in Australia, visit **www.fta.org.au**

4. AVOID CIRCUSES WHERE WILD ANIMALS ARE USED

The life of a circus animal is often not a happy one. Many animals, such as bears, lions, tigers and elephants, originally came from the wild and are mistreated to get them to perform. Well, it's not natural for animals to balance things on their heads and ride on tricycles – not unless it's a cartoon.

To get them to perform for audiences, their so-called trainers tend to use two methods – punishment and deprivation. Animals are beaten if they won't perform and are starved. They might have tight collars put on them, be subjected to electric shocks and cattle prods, and be jabbed with metal hooks that tear through their skin.

Their sad plight doesn't end there. Circus animals are often kept in cramped cages without enough space and are not adequately exercised or fed. They may be forced to eat and sleep in the same cage where they do the toilet.

fact

Circuses often get away with mistreating their animals because training sessions aren't monitored by animal welfare bodies. The only way people know what goes on, is because animal charities like PETA have recorded undercover footage.

fact

In the UK, British politicians voted to ban the use of wild animals in circuses. In some UK towns and cities, circuses with wild animals were already banned.

fact

Circuses can be entertaining without any animals being used. Think of the Big Top and you think of trapeze artists flying through the air and clowns soaking people with water hidden in their bowties.

5. DON'T VACATION OR BUY PROPERTIES IN COUNTRIES WHERE THERE ARE HUMAN RIGHTS ABUSES LIKE SAUDI ARABIA

Did you know that there is a country where women are not allowed to drive and if they do they can be thrown in prison? Where punishments for theft can mean limbs being amputated? And, if you are considered to be a 'sexual deviant,' which can mean anything from being homosexual to sharing a room with a member of the opposite sex you are not married to, you can be flogged?

For all its glorious beaches and luxurious hotels, Saudi Arabia is a country accused of the worst kind of human rights abuses by Amnesty International and Human Rights Watch. The country doesn't have a democracy; what it does have is a ruling royal family.

Women are not treated as equals to men. They're not allowed to vote. A guardian system is also in place whereby women are not allowed to do things we all take for granted, like accepting employment, getting married, buying or selling a house, studying or even traveling without the permission of a male guardian, who can be a father, husband or brother.

Despite the country's human rights abuses, it's seen as a dream destination for a vacation and an ideal place to own a holiday property. Saudi Arabia isn't alone in not treating its citizens and immigrant workers fairly.

"Service to others is the rent you pay for your room here on earth."

Muhammad Ali

fact

Dubai in the United Arab Emirates is considered another dream vacation spot because of its beautiful beaches. The country's estimated 250,000 foreign laborers who built most of the properties wouldn't think so. According to Human Rights Watch, conditions they live in are described as 'less than human.'

fact

It was being ostracized from the international community and not being allowed to take part in sporting events that led to the end of apartheid in South Africa: a system whereby people were separated by race, with the black majority kept in poverty. You see, people power can make a difference.

6. DON'T GO TO THE DOGS (OR TO WATCH DOG RACING)

It's estimated that, in the UK, tens of thousands of greyhounds are killed each year for no other reason than they can't race any more or they weren't quite fast enough. The average age that greyhounds retire at is less than three years old as this is when they start to lose their speed. As a result of this, many greyhounds end up in need of new homes if they're not euthanized (killed).

The risk of injuries to racing dogs is very high. Many dogs end up crippled. Race fixing and dog doping also goes on and there have been cases of dogs being given cocaine.

There have been incidences in the UK where dogs that don't make it as racing dogs have been killed. In 2006, The Sunday Times newspaper in the UK, filmed two greyhound trainers taking two of their dogs who'd 'underperformed' to be shot dead by David Smith, who was dubbed the 'unofficial executioner' in the industry. The dog killer is said to have killed 10,000 greyhounds in 15 years. Both dogs were less than three-years-old and the trainers allegedly had them killed because a greyhound charity didn't have the space to take them for a week.

A court fined Smith, who used a bolt gun to kill the dogs, £2,000 not for killing the dogs as he broke no animal welfare laws, but because he didn't have a permit to bury them on his land. He left Durham Crown Court to a chorus of 'murderer' after being described as 'the greyhound serial killer.'

Greyhound trainers having their retired dogs killed is common place. Other dogs end up being taken in by charities. The majority of greyhounds were deliberately bred for racing.

fact

Live greyhound racing is banned in a number of American states. There are also a number of states where no racing takes place because there isn't the demand or desire for it.

tip

Throughout the USA, Canada and Europe (including the UK) there are retired greyhounds needing good homes. Go to **www.adopt-a-greyhound.org/directory/list.cfm** for a list. You can select by country.

The Retired Greyhound Trust in the UK are constantly on the look out for homes for unwanted dogs. Visit **www.retiredgreyhounds.co.uk** for details.

fact

Greyhounds make perfect family pets: they're laid back, gentle and good with children. They will chase cats though.

7. WRITE A LETTER FOR AMNESTY INTERNATIONAL

The whole reason that Amnesty International came into being was to protect and defend human rights throughout the world. One of the ways they do this is by getting people like you to write letters to politicians on behalf of victims of human rights abuses. Many of these victims are political prisoners who are locked away in conditions that many of us would find barbaric and some are tortured.

This is often for no other reason than they disagree with the government of the time, usually because of how they treat people.

The organization has a global presence and has many different campaigns running at one time.

For more details, visit the relevant site:
www.amnestyusa.org
www.amnesty.ca
www.amnesty.org/en/region/south-africa
http://amnesty.org.uk
www.amnesty.org.au

fact

For many prisoners, getting a letter is the only contact they have with the outside world. It lets them know that they haven't been abandoned.

tip

Avoid discussing politics and instead concentrate on things like what your daily life is like. Avoid depressing subjects, too.

8. BUY PRODUCTS FROM CRUELTY FREE FASHION DESIGNERS

Stella McCartney is famous for her no fur and no leather stance in her designs, whilst companies like Calvin Klein and Herve Leger have strict no fur policies.

The reverse also applies: don't buy from designers who favor fur, like Burberry, Fendi, Gucci and Pucci.

Note – leather isn't considered cruelty free. This is because the animals it comes from (usually cows) are killed. This makes leather similar to fur in that the animals are killed to produce it.

tip

If you decide to boycott any companies because of their pro-fur stance, write to them and tell them why you are not buying their product.

It's not just fur that you need to look out for if you want to buy cruelty free fashion:

1. For anyone who loves horses, the prospect of ponies being sent to the slaughterhouse where they are killed and then skinned, will seem repugnant. Yet this does happen. Pony leather is used in handbags, shoes and purses.

2. Kangaroo leather – after hearing how kangaroos were slaughtered to make soccer (football) boots, David Beckham switched to boots made from synthetic materials instead.

3. Snakes and lizards are also killed so their skin can be turned into shoes, handbags and belts.

4. Seal skin is a kind of fur and may be used for outer garments, like coats, gloves and mufflers.

5. Alligators, which should be in the wild, are farmed so they can be killed for their skin.

6. There have been cases where cat and dog skin has been found in leather. This is believed to have come from animals slaughtered in China.

tip

Fur favoring companies change all the time, so it's always best to check.

Leather is never labeled, so you never know what animal it came from and how they were treated.

Faux or fake fur and leather can look as good as the real thing, but it's cheaper to buy and cruelty free.

9. LOOK OUT FOR YOUR NEIGHBORS

We've all read stories about people who have passed away in their own homes and their bodies have been left undiscovered until someone complained about the smell. We've all shook our heads and thought how terrible that was. But, how many of us have decided that, from now on, we'll check up our neighbors to make sure they're doing okay and don't need help with something like getting groceries in and walking the dog?

Loneliness is one of the cruelest things there is.

The next time you cook or bake something and have some to spare, why not go round to your neighbor's. It's the neighborly thing to do. Or take in their mail when they are out. Small gestures like this help build relationships.

Why not start a neighborhood watch? All the neighbors could get together say once every two weeks for drinks and nibbles and discuss any concerns they have. You could take it in turns to host the meeting.

Have a street party. Perfect for getting to know the neighbors.

"Wherever a man turns he can find someone who needs him."

Albert Schweitzer

10. DON'T DO SHARK CAGE DIVING/BAITING

This is where you go inside a shark proof cage and are lowered into the water. You may throw in food to get the sharks to come to you. Although the sharks are not harmed in any way, marine biologists believe that this new craze causes sharks to see human beings as food because they become acquainted with the scent. Sharks are then killed when they attack or there seems to be a threat of them attacking.

Think of it a bit like this. There's a lion in a cage and humans are dangled in front of that lion. There's no chance of the lion getting the people, but then one day the lion escapes and, because it was tantalized by the smell of humans, it goes and eats one. The lion ends up being killed for just doing what comes naturally.

fact

There has been an increase in shark attacks. Animal behaviorists believe this is linked to the popularity of shark cage diving.

11. DONATE YOUR OLD GLASSES TO CHARITY

Can you think what it would be like to be unable to see? Some charities have a scheme whereby you donate your old glasses or spectacles and they are given to someone less fortunate so they can see.

As well as raising money to buy prescription glasses for people who can't afford them in the USA, New Eyes for the Needy also give donated glasses to people in need abroad. Movie star Jake Gyllenhaal is a supporter of the organization that has helped over 7million people to see again.

Visit **www.neweyesfortheneedy.org** for details, including how to ship your glasses. They also accept hearing aids, jewelry and giftware to raise funds.

tip

The Lions Club International have Lions Eyeglass Recycling Centers (LERCs) located around the world – the USA, Australia, Canada, France, Italy, South Africa and Spain. Glasses collected are then sorted through by volunteers. Find out more at their site **www.lionsclubs.org/EN/our-work/sight-programs/eyeglass-recycling/lions-eyeglass-recycling-centers.php**

tip

If you live in the UK, you can take your old glasses along to Vision Express and many other opticians, including independent opticians, and they will be passed along to Vision Aid Overseas. The ones they collect go to people in the Third World. Read more about the scheme at **www.vao.org.uk/showpage.php?id=230**

12. DON'T BUY PUPPIES FROM PUPPY MILLS (ALSO CALLED PUPPY FARMS)

To feed the huge demand for puppies, more and more puppy mills are opening up. In these places, the mother dogs are usually kept in a confined space (usually a cage) in converted barns or sheds, often for 24 hours a day with no access to the outdoors.

They have one litter of puppies and are then bred again and again until they are too old to have any puppies.

In a nutshell, puppy mills are the factory farming of dogs. As with factory farming of cattle, little attention is paid to the welfare of the dogs. The most important thing to the owners of these places is making as much money as possible from as little outlay as possible. This means making as many puppies as possible even if it's detrimental to the welfare of the mother dogs.

There are a number of reasons why you should never buy a puppy from one of these places:

- Many end up being killed when they become too tired or old to breed and outlive their usefulness.

- During their difficult lives, mother dogs may never see daylight and may have to lie on the same bedding they have to do the toilet on because they are never allowed to go outside. The reason they are not allowed out is because it means less work for the people who are employed by these farms. Employees tend to be untrained and poorly paid.

- Often minimum welfare standards are not even met for the mother dogs and their puppies. The mothers can become ill and so can their puppies, through lack of proper nutrition, sunlight and infections caused by dirty environments.

- It's more likely that a puppy bought from a puppy mill will be sickly or even have to be put down than a puppy bought from a breeder who breeds dogs in their own home. It's very common for the owners of these places to be sued when people take home their puppies and discover they have illnesses caused by inbreeding, poor hygiene standards and poor nutrition.

- Puppy mills puppies often have behavioral problems because they have not been properly socialized. This means they can be very aggressive or go the other way and be timid to the point where they are scared of everything, including people.

HOW TO AVOID BUYING FROM PUPPY MILLS

Despite the shocking stories, many people still continue to give money to puppy mills without even realizing it.

Here are some tips to help you avoid unwittingly buying a puppy from a puppy mill or puppy farm:

- Always ask to see the puppy in its home environment and never agree to meet anyone who is selling a puppy in a public place, like a car park.

- Ask the breeder questions and ask to visit. Any reputable breeder will expect this. It's the ones who seem tight lipped or reluctant for you to visit who might be the ones with puppy mills.

- Make sure you see the puppy with the rest of the litter and, if possible, see the father. Does the puppy look lively and healthy?

- Puppies should come with paperwork. This should show whether they have been vaccinated and have been to see a vet. Many breeders make sure puppies are vaccinated before they are found new homes. They should have also been wormed as all puppies are born with worms. This is natural.

- Get a dog by word of mouth from someone you know well and trust. Most puppies from puppy mills are advertised on the Internet and in local newspapers and shops windows. Buyers are unaware of where they come from.

- Never buy a dog from a pet shop. There is a good chance the ones they sell come from puppy mills. Some pet super stores may also sell puppies from puppy mills.

- If the seller wants to sell you the puppy before its eight weeks old, you should be concerned. Puppies should stay with their mothers until they are at least eight weeks old. This is to ensure they get enough nutrients from their mother's milk.

- Try and see your puppy on at least two different visits before you take it home. Responsible breeders won't mind if you do this.

fact

Since the 1980s, the Humane Society of the United States has been fighting to shut down puppy mills as they believe they are cruel and inhumane.

fact

Most of the puppy mills in the UK are in Wales and Ireland. In Ireland, puppy farms are not regulated.

fact

The conditions in some puppy mills are so bad that, if you kept your pet dog in those conditions, you would probably be prosecuted for animal cruelty.

tip

Why not adopt an unwanted dog? All over the world, dogs are put down for no other reason than they don't have a home. This problem is made worse by the demand for puppies, usually pedigree ones, many of whom end up in animal shelters and with charities as unwanted pets. Wherever you live, there will be an animal shelter near you.

tip

There are also dogs that need to be fostered. This is where people are needed to temporarily look after a dog when their owner can't look after them for a period of time for some reason, say they are in hospital or moving into accommodation for a short period of time that doesn't allow pets. Animal charities may also need foster carers for animals that need to finish a course of medical treatment before they are given new homes.

tip

Animal shelters also need dog walkers and people to clean out kennels. Why not volunteer?

" Charity sees the need, not the cause. "

German Proverb

13. TEACH ADULTS HOW TO READ AND WRITE

What could exclude people from society more than them not being able to read or write? Literacy problems can stop you from doing a lot of things, like getting a job (how can you fill in the application form, far less write a résumé / CV), enjoying a good book and even go shopping (reading packaging would be impossible).

The good news is that there are adult literacy classes that can help and you could be making a real difference by volunteering to be a tutor.

In the USA, in order to get citizenship, applicants have to pass a simple reading and writing exam as well as learn about American history and culture. Many of these people go to literacy and citizenship classes to learn and these classes need volunteers to help students. Ask your local college or search **www.literacydirectory.org** for details of adult literacy classes near you, then contact the learning institutions and ask if they need volunteers.

Canada

In Canada, there are adult literacy classes too. Search **www.nald.ca** They also have an organization called Teachers on Wheels that needs volunteers to act as one to one tutors. Instead of in a classroom, tutoring takes place wherever it is convenient for the tutor and pupil. For details go to **www.nald.ca/tow**

UK

In the UK, there are colleges and community learning centers offering classes to help people of all abilities improve their reading and writing skills. These classes need volunteers to assist teachers. Qualifications aren't needed, but you may be given some training which could even lead to a qualification. Some of the classes are aimed at people who have newly arrived in the country.

Australia

Asylum Seekers Centers need volunteer teachers. See **www. refugeecouncil.org.au/getinvolved/volunteer.html** for more information on that and other possible volunteer opportunities.

WOULD YOU MAKE A GOOD TEACHER?

Before you volunteer, ask yourself:

- Do you have the patience and understanding needed to be a good teacher?

- Do you have good listening skills?

- Are your English skills good, or do you have problems with your spelling? If so, it might not be a good idea to become a teacher.

- If the person you are helping can speak little English, will you still be able to make yourself understood? This is the key to being a good teacher.

- Can you get on well with people from all backgrounds and ages? You will be assigned pupils.

- Do you think you could motivate someone to learn, including encouraging them to persevere when things aren't going well?

- Do you have the time to devote to helping someone? There's no point in you volunteering to help someone and then stopping classes because you have other commitments, as tutoring will often be on a one on one basis.

tip

Have you considered teaching English to those who speak another language? This can be extremely rewarding and the good news is that teachers are wanted all around the world. As well as helping people and earning some money, you may get the chance to travel. This is called

Teaching English as a Foreign language, or TEFL, and you will need to undergo very detailed training first. You would have to pay for the training.

To read more about it, go to **www.tefl.com** They have a list of available jobs throughout the world.

14. DON'T ATTEND OR BET ON THE THREE DAY ENGLISH GRAND NATIONAL EVENT

Imagine a sporting event where participants die. Should it still go on? Would it still go on?

Between 2000 and 2011, 20 horses have died on the world famous Grand National course at Aintree in Liverpool in the UK. 9 of those deaths were in the big race and the other 11 were on shorter races that are run on the same course during the first two days of the three day race meeting.

There is no official record of the total number of horses that have died in the big race as it is not good for the horse racing community.

fact

In the 2011 National, two horses died in the four-and-a-half mile steeplechase race – Ornais at the fourth jump (broken neck) and Dooneys Gate (with a broken back) at notorious Becher's Brook. The course had to be changed to avoid people seeing the two dead horses being removed. The horse that won the race, Ballabriggs, was seriously dehydrated at the end and was close to collapse. Three of the top four finishing horses were so exhausted they didn't make it into the winners enclosure.

Following the event, there were calls for the race to be banned.

Animal Aid director Andrew Tyler blamed the tightly packed and often high fences over a long course for making it so dangerous. 'The public has been conned into believing that the Grand National is a great sporting spectacle when, in reality, it is straightforward animal abuse that is on a par with Spanish bullfighting.'

tip

The horse racing industry is a cruel one. Horses that don't make it are often destroyed.

15. SPONSOR A CHILD ABROAD

You could make a real difference to a child's life and all for a little money per day. The money raised from sponsorship goes towards not just your child's education and their future, but will also benefit the whole community.

America

If you live in America, you could sponsor a child with World Vision. In doing so, you could help bring fresh water to that child's community. Children are from a number of different countries and you get to choose who you sponsor or the site will come up with a child for you.
For details, visit – **www.worldvision.org**

Canada

Canada has its own organization for sponsoring children abroad. Plan is one of the oldest and largest international development agencies and they say they 'are independent and inclusive of all faiths and cultures.'
For details, go to **http://plancanada.ca/childsponsorship**

UK

For UK residents, you can sponsor a child through Action Aid. Under the scheme, you can sponsor someone from a variety of countries, including Brazil, Peru, Haiti, Ethiopia, India and China amongst others. You'll get an update on your child's progress, a picture and can also write to the child you sponsor. In certain cases, you may even be allowed to visit the child you are sponsoring, by arrangement with the charity who will make sure a support worker can go with you. Go to
www.actionaid.org.uk/102425/sponsor_a_child.html for more details.

You could also sponsor a child through Save The Children **www. savethechildren.org/site/c.8rKLIXMGIpI4E/b.6146367/k.8EA1/ Sponsor_A_Child.htm** They need people to sponsor children in America because one in five children in the country live in poverty.

Australia

If you're thinking of sponsoring a child in Australia, visit this site for details – **http://trans.worldvision.com.au/default.aspx**

`tip`

Remember, there will be children in your own country needing help too. Donate unwanted clothes, food and toys to charity, including unwanted presents.

16. DON'T FLY WITH AIRLINES WHO TRANSPORT MONKEYS TO ANIMAL RESEARCH LABS

In 2011, funnyman Ricky Gervais joined the British Union for the Abolition of Vivisection (BUAV) Cargo Cruelty campaign against the shipping of monkeys by airlines to research labs. The monkeys destined for these labs are taken from the wild, or they are the offspring of those taken from the wild. They are being sent to labs in the USA, UK, Japan and Europe where they will be experimented on and are usually kept in conditions that any pet owner would be prosecuted for if they did the same.

To find out more, go to **www.buav.org/cargocruelty**

Their site also has a list of airlines who fly monkeys to research labs and ones who don't, if you go to the link and then scroll down until you see 'find out which airlines still transport primates for research.' Note – this list is constantly updated and you may find some airlines bow to public pressure and stop transporting monkeys.

" I was shocked to learn that some airlines transport monkeys to laboratories around the world. I support the BUAV's Cargo Cruelty campaign and urge these airlines to take a compassionate stance and say no to monkey shipments. "

Ricky Gervais

fact

The monkeys are placed in tiny cramped cages in cargo holds, mainly on passenger flights.

tip

If you decide not to fly with an airline because they transport monkeys to laboratories, write to them and tell them why.

17. BE A GOOD SAMARITAN

There is a way that you can help create a more compassionate world without it costing a cent. All it takes is being nice and considerate and thinking of others.

How about:

- Taking the time to smile and say 'hello' to strangers you see on the street. A friendlier world is a happier world and a happier world is a more compassionate world.

- Is there a soup kitchen in your area where they feed the homeless? If so, why not ask if they need volunteers to work in it or donations of food?

- Send a care parcel to a soldier stationed abroad. Imagine what it must be like for them miles away from home and all the comforts it brings. If you're a UK citizen go to **http://www.supportoursoldiers. co.uk/irshop.aspx?section=content&page=115** for info. There are also links to other sites aimed at sending parcels to personnel in other branches of the military, including **www.anysailor.com** and **www.anymarine.com** If you live in the UK, go to **www. supportoursoldiers.co.uk** for details. They also have a list of suggested items to include.

18. BUY DOG OR CAT FOOD THAT HASN'T BEEN TESTED ON ANIMALS

It may sound ridiculous, but many pet food companies test their food on lab or kennel animals. This is so they can make certain health claims like 'this food will increase your ageing dog's mobility.'

These dogs are usually kept in a lab or a kennel environment and often undergo invasive testing. It's not simply a matter of them being given the food to eat and treated like pets. And, even when they are well looked after, they are denied the right to live a normal life as companion animals and to indulge in normal behaviors.

fact

There have been documented cases where the treatment these animals have received has fallen way short of animal welfare standards. One well known company debarked dogs (debarking is a veterinary surgery that involves removing tissue from the dog's vocal chords so that a dog's bark is merely a whisper), placed animals in barren cages and removed muscles from dogs' legs (they did this so they could say their food strengthened muscles).

If pet owners did the same, they would be prosecuted.

tip

If you want to know for certain whether a certain brand of dog or cat food is tested on lab or kenneled animals, ask the company who makes it. Ask them whether they or their suppliers use invasive tests on animals and or keep them in labs or kennels. Make them aware of the fact that there is no need to do that as pet foods can be tested on animals in their own homes under the watchful eyes of their owners. Also make them aware of the fact that you'll only buy dog food tested in the more humane way.

fact

The US Department of Agriculture investigated a complaint by PETA in 2006 about invasive testing of Procter & Gamble's IAMS brand. This followed an undercover investigation by PETA, which was well documented in the press. The USDA agreed with PETA that the laboratory had failed to provide veterinary care and pain relief to suffering animals who were also not given sufficient space. There were 40 other violations of the federal Animal Welfare Act in total.

tip

Be wary of pet food that makes new claims like 'improves muscle tone.' To back up new claims they will probably have tested the food on lab animals.

fact

In America, the UK and the EU, PETA have a scheme that requires pet food companies not to directly fund lab animal testing or any tests on animals that are cruel and harmful. Go to **www.peta.com** (or one of the different sites listed on the home page) for details and put 'non-animal tested companion animal food' in the search box. They have a list of ethical companies who do non-invasive food testing on animals in their own homes. These companies are given what's called '*PETA* Statement of Assurance.'

fact

In the UK, the BUAV used to have a No Animal Testing Pet Food Standard, whereby companies that didn't test their pet food on lab animals were granted their seal of approval. This no longer exists.

tip

To find out whether the food you give your pet is not tested on lab animals, visit the Uncaged website at **www.uncaged.co.uk**

" *I've learned that you shouldn't go through life with a catcher's mitt on both hands; you need to be able to throw something back.* **"**

Maya Angelou, baseball star

19.THINK ABOUT BEING A SAMARITAN OR VOLUNTEER COUNSELOR

Sometimes we just need someone to talk to about our problems; a person who will listen and not judge us.

The Samaritans operate 24 hours a day, seven days a week and offer a number you can phone to talk to someone. You don't need to book an appointment or phone between office hours. Anything callers tell the Samaritans is completely confidential.

COULD YOU BE A SAMARITAN?

- Are you over 18 years of age?

- Are you a good listener? It can be a difficult skill to master. Many of us talk too much and don't listen enough.

- Are you easily shocked? You may hear things that you have never heard before.

- Are you open minded and tolerant of people from all walks of life?

- Can you listen to people without making any snap judgments?

- Would you be able to listen to people's problems without telling them what they should do? Samaritans and counselors are there to listen, not to give people advice.

For more details of becoming a volunteer, visit your country's website.

Note – Canada and Australia don't have the Samaritans, but they will have other similar charities that need volunteer counselors. Why not volunteer?

America

In America, the Samaritans are called Samaritans USA and they have professional and volunteer-run public education programs, as well as hotlines people can phone for help.
For more details, visit **www.samaritansusa.org**

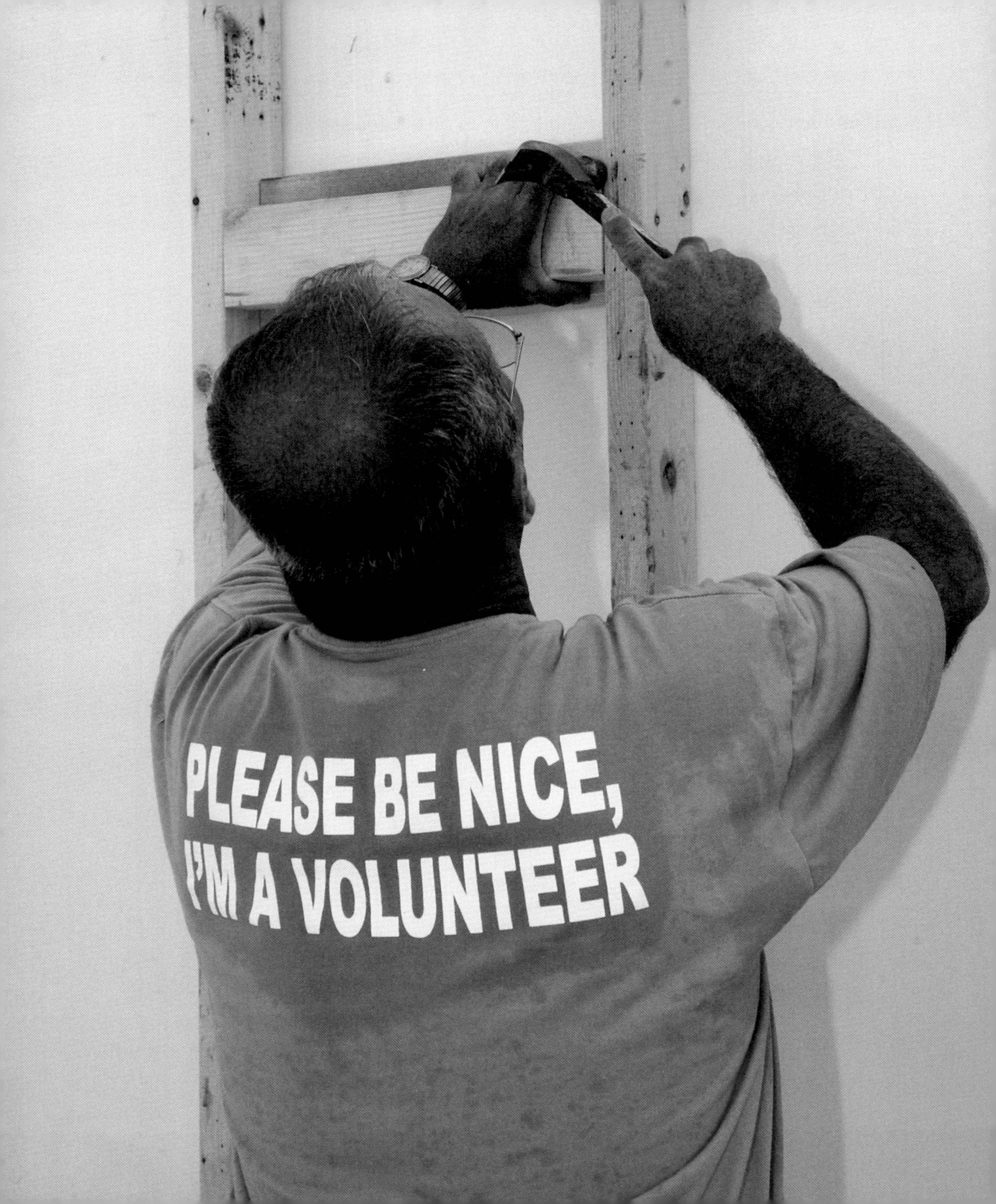
PLEASE BE NICE,
I'M A VOLUNTEER

tip

There are also what's known as suicide prevention hotlines who need volunteers. To find them visit the **www.befrienders.org** home page and, just below the menu bar, go to 'find a Helpline by country' and select the country you are in. Often these hotlines are short of volunteers, especially around Christmas time and Thanksgiving, when people are particularly prone to depression.

UK & Republic of Ireland

Their site has a 'find your nearest branch' function on the home page. Visit **www.samaritans.org**

To find out how to volunteer, go to your nearest branch.

tip

Many colleges and schools have volunteer counselors (often called outreach counselors) who will speak to students experiencing problems like bullying and peer pressure. These counselors are usually students themselves who live on campus.

tip

If you don't live in the USA, the UK or Ireland and want details of your nearest hotline (helpline), visit **www.befrienders.org**

If you phone up or email and ask about volunteering, someone will help you.

Become a Cruelty Free Crusader

" *Change is not made without inconvenience even from worse to better.* *"*

Samuel Johnson

Chapter 8
Become a Cruelty Free Crusader

At times it may seem like there is nothing we can do that can even make a dent in the cruelty in this world, whether its people forced into slave labor or animals being immobilized so they can have poison dripped into their eyes. But the truth is, we all have more power than we realize.

You see, companies want your money. They want you to buy their products. And, if enough people won't buy from them because they use practices the public considers unacceptable, and those non-buyers make it clear exactly why they won't buy, these companies will change their ways.

STAY INFORMED

Being informed is the key to being a cruelty free crusader.

If you want to know about companies who don't use cruelty free practices as well as those that do, you need to keep updated. As well as the organizations mentioned in other chapters, here are a few organizations that can help.

Note – Most of those listed are aimed at helping the rights of workers, as animal welfare charities have already been covered in previous chapters.

- Clean Clothes Campaign (CCC) – Their aim is to improve the working conditions of garment workers throughout the world. They do this by trying to make sure that consumers like you are kept informed. They are based in Europe, but they also work with similar organizations in the USA, Canada and Australia. Read more about them and their campaigns at **www.cleanclothes.org**

- Labour Behind the Label also support the rights of garment workers and aims to improve the working conditions of all workers by publicizing their cause, pressurizing companies who use labor into making sure workers are treated fairly, supporting workers as they battle for decent pay and conditions, as well as campaigning to get governments to ensure better treatment for workers. Read more at **www.labourbehindthelabel.org**

- **www.change.org** describes itself as an 'online activism platform for social change that raises awareness about important causes and connects people to opportunities for powerful action.' You can use their site to organize you own campaign and set up a petition. Previous campaigns include helping to get Chinese dissident artist Ai Weiwei out of prison, getting Hilary Clinton to support the women's right to drive campaign in Saudi Arabia (women were banned from driving in the country) and the toughening up of animal cruelty laws in Canada prompted by 100 sled dogs being brutally killed in British Columbia.

- Greenpeace wants to save the planet. Read more about them and their campaigns at **www.greenpeace.org/international/en/**

- Although they are based in the UK, Oxfam are a global organization. Go to **www.oxfam.org.uk** to hear about the work they are doing and their current campaigns.

- The Born Free Foundation is a worldwide animal conservation charity whose aims are to stop individual animal suffering and to protect endangered species in the wild. Visit **www.bornfree.org.uk** to see their current campaigns.

tip

If you're on Facebook, Twitter or any other social networking site, follow, friend or like the organizations on them.

tip

Are you a sports fan? Ask your favorite club what they do to ensure that official merchandise is made by workers who are treated fairly. Sportswear is one area where workers can be exploited.

USE TECHNOLOGY TO KEEP OTHER PEOPLE INFORMED

The good thing about the Internet is that it has never been so easy to get your message across. Using social media, like Facebook, Twitter and Myspace, as well as blogs and message boards, is the key.

Say you tweet about a product to 600 of your followers on Twitter. Then a few of those people read your tweet and decide to retweet it. Add all the people together who have read what you've had to say and your audience could run into the thousands.

tip

You could also start a Facebook page or group and see if you can attract anyone else who feels like you do. Use a name that makes your cause clear, i.e. Axe Child Labor, Live Cruelty Free or Ban Sweatshops.

START A PETITION

There are also petition sites where you can upload a petition, say asking for a company not to sell fur or to make sure their workers are paid fairly.

Petition sites:

- www.gopetition.com has petitions for over 70 countries and was ranked as the top petition site by Google in 2010.

- www.onlinepetition.com – With this one you can attach blog posts to your petition.

- www.ipetitions.com has attracted millions of signatures on a variety of topics.

Watch out for petition sites that offer to pay you a small fee for every signature. Those sites are aimed at collecting names and emails for spammers and go against the spirit of petitions, namely to express your views and not to cash in.

Petition tips:

1. When writing an online petition, its best if you are short and to the point. Look at other petitions to see how it's done.

2. Petitions must have an aim, i.e. 'the undersigned want current laws changed so that non-essential animal testing will be banned.'

3. You don't need to be emotional, as the facts should speak for themselves.

4. You can add links to information in your petition, so people can read about the facts themselves.

5. Allow everyone who signs to be anonymous if they want to be. This will dispel their fears that you may be just trying to get their details to sell on to spammers.

6. Post links to the petition on your website, blog, Twitter, Facebook and any other networks you use. You need to get the word out. You can also use the link to the petition as your signature in an email. Make sure it's your personal one though and not your work, as your employers may object. You can also create a badge on Facebook.

tip

Don't forget to send a tweet or message to the company themselves. Let them know what potential customers like you think. Companies have no way of knowing people's thoughts unless people tell them.

EXPRESS YOUR VIEWS

You've just watched a documentary exposing a store that you shop in as one that uses underpaid labor. You're shocked, you always thought it was a pretty good store. How do you let the company know how you feel about their lack of ethics?

- Write a letter to their HQ. Try and get a named person to send it to, so it doesn't get lost. This should be someone like the managing director, chief executive or a director.

- Write to newspaper and magazine letter pages telling them what you think.

- Write your own petition and collect as many signatures as you can and then either send it in or go along with a group of friends. Try and get your local newspaper to cover you presenting the petition. You may have to make an appointment with the company beforehand.

- Send an email detailing your concerns. No personal abuse.

tip

Whether a letter or in an email, the best sorts of communications are the ones that start with something like 'as a lifelong shopper in your store/buyer of your products, I was upset to find out that…'. If you want companies to act more responsibly towards human beings and animals, you need to make them think that they will be losing valuable customers like you if they don't change their ways.

" Unless someone like you cares a whole awful lot, nothing is going to get better. It's not. "

Dr. Seuss

Bottom line – companies care about making money, that's all. If they think they will lose money they will change the way they operate to maintain their profits.

It may also help if you say that you have heard a rival company is more ethical and you will shop there from now on. Companies hate the thought of losing customers to their rivals.

ATTEND A PEACEFUL PROTEST

Did you know that there are countries where the government and companies can do whatever they want, yet people are not allowed to protest?

If you're lucky enough to live in America, Canada, Australia or the UK, the good news is that you are allowed to protest as long as you abide by the law.

Friends of the Earth have a free PDF document called 'How to protest on the right side of the law in the UK.' Not only does the document offer advice on how to stay on the right side of the law, there's also tips on how to make sure your protest has the right kind of impact. **www.foe.co.uk/ resource/how_tos/cyw_59_protest_law.pdf**

HOW TO ORGANIZE A PEACEFUL PROTEST

The key to any successful protest is organization.

- Check with the police and your local council to find out if you need some kind of permit or permission to have the protest.

- Decide beforehand what you want to say. What is your message? This could be that you want people to boycott a certain store because they sell something, like sandblasted jeans (workers in the factories that make them have died because they've ingested the silicon used to give them that sand blasted effect), fur or Foie gras. If you get stuck, think 'what is my objective/aim or what do I want to achieve?'

- Decide beforehand what kind of protest it's going to be and where it will take place. Will you protest outside a store or an organization? Will you protest in a town square or outside a shopping mall? Will it be a silent protest or will there be chants?

- Discuss what you'll do if the protest gets out of hand, as some protests do attract troublemakers. For that reason, try wherever possible to only include people you or your friends know in the protest.

- Make up leaflets so that, if people want to know why you are protesting, you have something to give them. Who knows, they may even join the protest.

- Arrange a meet up place for everyone involved. That way you don't end up with confusion.

- Publicize the protest. Use local newspapers, cable stations and radio stations, use social networking, like Facebook (maybe set up a page or group) and Twitter. The more people who know the more people who might turn up. Also try and write in to local newspapers and radio and cable channels, too. Maybe they will be interested in interviewing you?

- Make up banners and posters to take with you. Make the message as short and clear as possible. For instance, 'No to animal testing' or 'No to using child labor.'

- Make sure that everyone knows that this is a peaceful protest and that participants shouldn't behave in a threatening or confrontational way.

- Could you line up a celebrity or high profile supporter to speak at the protest? This will get the media interested in your protest.

tip

Protests should be carried out on public land wherever possible. If you protest on private land, you may get arrested for trespass.

tip

If a store security guard asks you to move away, you should ask where the store's land ends, because you have the right to protest on the public highway.

tip

Be careful that your behavior, or that of any of the protestors, doesn't cross the line and become a criminal offence. This could mean harassing someone by making them feel threatened by you or your presence or by trying to get them to do something they don't want to do.

fact

It was protests by the Suffragette movement that led to women getting the vote in the UK.

OTHER THINGS YOU CAN DO

- If a company doesn't sell a certain cruelty free product, say make up that's not tested on animals or Fair Trade coffee, ask for it. Get your friends to ask for it. The more people who ask, the more likely stores are to stock it.

- Try and shop in stores that sell Fair Trade goods. Things like Fair Trade coffee and bananas are widely available. The more people who buy them, the greater the demand, and there will be more farmers and workers who are paid a fair wage for their produce.

- Ask stores why their clothing is so cheap. Who makes the garments and how do they make sure no child labor or slave labor is used? Where are the clothes made? Do they have any literature showing workers making them?

Useful Websites

The following websites are a good source of information for those looking to live a more compassionate life. They cover a variety of things, like buying Fair Trade and cosmetics that aren't tested on animals.

Note – their inclusion here is in no way an endorsement of the site and its contents. Sites are listed for guidance only.

ANIMAL CHARITIES

www.aspca.org
The American Society for the Prevention of Cruelty to Animals.

www.animalaid.org.uk
Animal Aid is based in the UK. They highlight the plight of animals, including in cruel sports like horse racing and pheasant shooting.

www.awlnsw.com.au
Animal Welfare League New South Wales. As well as campaigning on behalf of animals in Australia, they also have cats and dogs needing new homes.

www.spcamontreal.com
The Canadian Society for the Prevention of Cruelty to Animals (CSPCA) was the first humane society in Canada and was founded in 1869.

www.dogstrust.org.uk
Dogs Trust (UK) never put a healthy dog down.

www.humanesociety.org
The Humane Society of the United States.

www.peta.org/index_landing.asp
PETA (people for the Ethical Treatment of Animals) operates worldwide.

www.petrescue.com.au
Pet Rescue tries to find homes for unwanted pets in Australia.

www.rspca.org.uk/freedomfood
The Royal Society for the Protection of Cruelty to Animals run the Freedom Food scheme in the UK.

www.viva.org.uk
Viva (Vegetarians International Voice for Animals).

ANTI-VIVISECTION ORGANIZATIONS

Note – vivisection means experimenting on live animals.

www.aavs.org
American Anti-vivisection Society (AAVS).

www.ad-international.org
Animal Defenders International are a global organization who also campaign to replace animal experiments.

http://animal-lib.org.au
Animal Liberation has branches in all states of Australia and many thousands of supporters.

www.buav.org
British Union for the Abolition of Vivisection (BUAV).

www.drhadwentrust.org
Not only do they campaign against animal experiments, they actively fund alternatives.

www.four-paws.org.uk
Four Paws works to end all animal suffering and helps all creatures great and small.

www.navs.org.uk
The National Anti-Vivisection Society is one of the oldest anti-vivisection organizations in the world.

www.uncaged.co.uk
Exposing animal cruelty, especially in labs.

http://vivisectionresearch.ca
They campaign against vivisection in Canada.

CHILDREN'S CHARITIES

www.loveourchildrenusa.org
This American charity wants to end violence against children if they are being bullied or assaulted by their own parents.

www.barnardos.org.au/barnardos/html
www.barnardos.org.uk
Barnados has projects that help children all over the world.

www.childrensdefense.org
The US-based Child's Defense Fund mission is to 'leave no child behind.'

www.oxfam.org.uk
Oxfam are based in the UK, but the work they do helps the poorest children in the world.

www.savethechildren.org.uk
www.savethechildren.org.au
www.savethechildren.ca
Save The Children are based in the UK but they help children throughout the world. They have websites in the UK, Australia and Canada.
Save the Children also run a program where you can sponsor a child in the USA – www.savethechildren.org/site/c.8rKLIXMGIpI4E/b.6153159/k.C8D5/USA.htm

www.soschildrensvillages.ca
SOS Children's Villages Canada takes care of children who've been orphaned or abandoned.

CRUELTY FREE COSMETICS & TOILETRIES

There are more companies than ever before offering cosmetics and toiletries where neither the ingredients nor the final products are tested on animals. It would take up too much space to list them, but these are the most reliable sites.

www.gocrueltyfree.org
The Leaping Bunny List allows you to search by product and country.

www.choosecrueltyfree.org.au
The number one site for Australians who want to go cruelty free.

www.aavs.org
To get to the Compassionate Shopping Guide on the American Anti-Vivisection Society site, go to the home page and click on 'Shop with compassion' on the top right hand side of the page.

www.vegansociety.com/afssearch.aspx?ad=677814
The Vegan Society does an 'animal free shopper' guide.

FAIR TRADE

Buying Fair Trade makes a real difference to people's lives.

www.fta.org.au
Fairtrade site for Australia and New Zealand.

www.fairtrade.org.uk
Home of Fairtrade in the UK.

http://fairtrade.ca
Fair Trade Canada.

www.transfairusa.org
Website for the Fair Trade Certification in the USA.

Note – In the UK, Australia and New Zealand it's called Fairtrade. In Canada and the USA, it's called Fair Trade, although they are the same thing.

www.ethicalconsumer.org/home.aspx
Site offering tips on how to be a more ethical shopper.

HUMAN RIGHTS CHARITIES

www.amnesty.org
Amnesty International are probably the most famous organization of its type in the world.

www.actionaid.org.uk/100084/other_actionaid_websites.html
Action Aid has one aim: to end poverty wherever it may be. They offer sponsor a child schemes and do various famine appeals. Go to the link to visit their various countries sites.

www.cartercenter.org
The Carter Center promotes human rights throughout the world and is based in Atlanta in the USA.

www.hrw.org
Human Rights Watch highlights human rights abuses all over the world.

www.msf.org
Medecins Sans Frontieres (it's French and translates as doctors without borders) is an international humanitarian aid organization that provides emergency medical assistance to populations in danger in several countries throughout the world.

VEGETARIAN & VEGAN ORGANIZATIONS

www.americanvegan.org

The American Vegan Society (AVS). Their site explains more about the vegan lifestyle. They have a quarterly subscriber only magazine, aptly called American Vegan.

www.americanvegetarian.org

The American Vegetarian Society. Their site has a list of verified vegetarian products on their home page.

www.navs-online.org

The North American Vegetarian Society NAVS. Founded in 1974, they want to not only offer advice to vegetarians in America and Canada, but to also educate people about vegetarianism. They founded World Vegetarian Day, which is celebrated on October 1st every year. They have a section on frequently asked questions, as well as tasty recipe ideas. On their site, down the left hand side, they have helpful topics, like FAQ, Food and recipes and Dining Out.

www.vegsoc.org

The Vegetarian Society UK. Established in 1847, they are the oldest vegetarian organization in the world. They aim to educate people about vegetarianism and to support vegetarians. They have a comprehensive advice and information section. On the home page, you can click on a number of options, including 'Info & Advice and 'Go Veggie & Why.'

www.vegansociety.com

The Vegan Society. The best place to go for advice on going vegan. Click on the cloud on the left hand side that reads 'Become a vegan' of the home page. They also produce an Animal Free Shopper. See home page and half way down 'Animal Free Shopper.'

www.vegetariantimes.com

Vegetarian Times. This is America's top selling vegetarian magazine and their website has an extensive 'vegetarian starter kit.' Go to the site and click www.vegetariantimes.com/2007/pdf/vegetarian_starter_kit.pdf and a pdf file will load.

www.viva.org.uk

Viva! are Vegetarians International Voice for Animals. Their website has advice on going veggie, including animal free recipes, as well as details of campaigns to improve animal welfare. They have menus for 'Going vegetarian' and 'Going Vegan' on the left hand side menu on the home page. They also have their own Viva! symbol for approved products and stores. See www.viva.org.uk/businesses/symbolholders.html for details.

www.ivu.org

IVU are The International Vegetarian Union. They have been promoting vegetarianism throughout the world since 1908.

http://veg-soc.org

The Australian Vegetarian Society has a free book available for download on their site called Go Vegetarian. You can also join them and receive the quarterly member's magazine, Health and Vegetarian Life.

http://www.vegetarian.org.nz/content

The New Zealand Vegetarian Society offers advice on how to live meat and fish free. You can send for a free information pack via their site.

Book List

Animal Liberation: The Definitive Classic of the Animal Movement, by Peter Singer, Published by Harper, ISBN 978-0061711305

Giving: How Each of Us Can Change the World, by Bill Clinton, Published by Knopf, ISBN 978-1615568093

How to be an Ethical Shopper: The Practical Guide to Buying What You Believe in, by Melissa Corkhill, Published by Impact Publishing Ltd, ISBN 978-1904601456

How to Cook Everything Vegetarian: Simple Meatless Recipes for Great Food, by Mark Bittman, Published by John Wiley & Sons, ISBN 978-0764524837

Random Acts of Kindness, by The Editors of Conari Press, Published by Conari Press, ISBN 978-1573248532

Skinny Bitch, by Rory Freedman & Kim Barnouin, Published by Running Press, ISBN 978-0762424931

The Better World Shopping Guide: Every Dollar Makes a Difference (Better World Shopping Guide: Every Dollar Can Make a Difference), by Ellis Jones, Published by New Society Publishers, ISBN 978-0865716803

The Good Deed Guide: Simple Ways to Make the World a Better Place by James Grace, Lisa Grace, Published by Quirk Books, ISBN 978-1931686334

The Kind Diet: A Simple Guide to Feeling Great, Losing Weight, and Saving the Planet, by Alicia Silverstone, Published by Rodale, ISBN 978-1609611354

Picture Credits

Index